MAHABHARATA WAR DID HAPPEN BUT WHEN?

ITIHASA OF ANCIENT BHARATAVARSHA

A stone sculpture depicting an episode from the Mahabharata.

B NANDA GOPAL

Chennai • Bangalore

CLEVER FOX PUBLISHING
Chennai, India

Published by CLEVER FOX PUBLISHING 2024
Copyright © B NANDA GOPAL 2024

All Rights Reserved.
ISBN: 978-93-67076-57-6

This book has been published with all reasonable efforts taken to make the material error-free after the consent of the author. No part of this book shall be used, reproduced in any manner whatsoever without written permission from the author, except in the case of brief quotations embodied in critical articles and reviews.

The Author of this book is solely responsible and liable for its content including but not limited to the views, representations, descriptions, statements, information, opinions and references ["Content"]. The Content of this book shall not constitute or be construed or deemed to reflect the opinion or expression of the Publisher or Editor. Neither the Publisher nor Editor endorse or approve the Content of this book or guarantee the reliability, accuracy or completeness of the Content published herein and do not make any representations or warranties of any kind, express or implied, including but not limited to the implied warranties of merchantability, fitness for a particular purpose. The Publisher and Editor shall not be liable whatsoever for any errors, omissions, whether such errors or omissions result from negligence, accident, or any other cause or claims for loss or damages of any kind, including without limitation, indirect or consequential loss or damage arising out of use, inability to use, or about the reliability, accuracy or sufficiency of the information contained in this book.

ABOUT THE AUTHOR

Shri B Nanda Gopal is a Banker by profession. He has done CAIIB and Certificate in Credit Officer course from Indian Institute of Banking and Finance (IIBF). He has over 13 years of experience in the Banking sector, working in Federal Bank since June 2011. Currently, he is posted as an Assistant Manager in Federal Bank. He has keen interest in ancient history of India and other civilizations of the world.

This educational book authored by him is his first book.

I dedicate this book to my parents Shri Varakur Sivaraman Balakrishnan and Shrimati Ramani Balakrishnan

TABLE OF CONTENTS

About the Author .... *iii*
Preface .... *vii*
Introduction .... *viii*
Background .... *x*

PART I: The Puranas and the Average Reign per Ruler Hypothesis............ 1

1. The Earliest Buddhist Shrine: Excavating The Birth Place Of The Buddha, Lumbini (Nepal) – R.a.e. Coningham, K.p. Achary And Others 2
2. The Age of Mahajanapadas (From 623 B.C. to 323 B.C.) 4
3. The Date of Mahabharata War As Per Puranas 14
4. Approximate Dating of Mahabharata War 20

PART II: Mahabharata Epic, a Historical account not Mythological 25

1. The Brahmi Script 26
2. The War. War Chariots and War Horses 36
3. The Gana – Sanghas Or Gana – Rajyas of Ancient Bharatavarsha 44
4. Coins of Ancient Bharatavarsha 51
5. The Magadh – Vajji War – a Mythological Narration of a Historical Event 59

PART III: From an Archaeological Perspective............................ 72

1. Iron Metallurgy in Ancient Bharatavarsha 73
2. Beginning of Iron Age in Bharatavarsha and its Mahabharata Connection 78

3. The Hastinapura Floods, Indraprastha And Kaushambi Excavations 84
4. The Sinauli Chariot..91

PART IV: From an Astrological Perspective 93
1. The Date of Mahabharata War As Per Vedanga Jyotisha and Kollam Andu 94

PART V: From a Geological Perspective, supported by Archaeological Evidence 104
1. The Saurashtra Stone Anchors – an Archaeological Survey of India Report 105
2. 16 Not 36 and Mausala Parva 109
3. 1177 B.C. Geological Upheavals Around the World and Not in Bharatavarsha? 115

Conclusion *120*
Bibliography... *121*

PREFACE

𝓑y end of July 2024, I gave a completion to my research on various topics which were intertwined to perfection. Thus, it made possible to write a book on one of my favourite topics of discussion, reflected in the book's title, which had intrigued me since my school days.

I have done my best to logically break down my arguments and hypothesis and use maps and other pictorial references wherever required to make it more appealing for readers.

Ancillary reason for writing this book:-

We do have a recorded ancient history of more than 1000 years 'Before Christ' and it is a proud one. No, it did not start from the Mauryas as we were taught in our childhood, but still had all hallmarks of an advanced civilization, namely:

1. Martial Prowess.
2. Literature, including sacred texts written in indigenously developed Brahmi Script.
3. Religion as a way of life with righteousness as its core.
4. Currency based trade instead of barter.
5. Iron Metallurgy, most advanced of its time, e.g. Wootz steel swords.
6. Earliest use of iron weapons.
7. Ancient Port and Harbour.

It is Itihasa of our Bharatavarsha. Take pride in it.

INTRODUCTION

*B*elow mentioned are excerpts from Adi Parva, the first of 18 parvas:

1. Chapter 3, Shloka 1
   जनमेजयः पारिक्षितः सह भरातृभिः कुरुक्षेत्रे दीर्घसत्त्रम उपास्ते तस्य भरातरस तरयः शरुतसेनोग्रसेनो भीमसेन इति

   Janamejaya, Parikshit with his brothers worships Dirghasatram at Kurukshetra. His brothers names are Sharutsena, Ugrasena and Bhimasena.

2. Chapter 3, Shloka 18
   तेनैवम उक्ता भरातरस तस्य तथा चक्रुः
   स तथा भरातृन संदिश्य तक्षशिलां परत्यभिपरतस्थे
   तं च देशं वशे सथापयाम आस

   He said so and his brothers did so. He thus instructed his brothers and set out for Takshashila and he subdued that country and established that country under his control.

3. Chapter 3, Shloka 179
   पुरा तक्षशिलातस तं निवृत्तम अपराजितम
   सम्यग विजयिनं दृष्ट्वा समन्तान मन्त्रिभिर वृतम

   In the past, he had withdrawn from Takshashila and was undefeated. Seeing him perfectly victorious, the ministers surrounded him from all sides.

4. Chapter 1, Introductory Shloka
   नारायणं नमस्कृत्य नरं चैव नरोत्तमम
   देवीं सरस्वतीं चैव ततो जयम उदीरयेत

   One should offer obeisance to Narayana, Nara the best of men and to Goddess Saraswati, and then chant Jaya.

5. Chapter1, Shloka 1
   लोमहर्षणपुत्र उग्रश्रवाः सूतः पौराणिको नैमिषारण्ये शौनकस्य कुलपतेर दवादशवार्षिके सत्रे

   Ugrasrava, the son of Lomharsana, the mythical charioteer at the twelfth annual session of the sages and patriarch Shaunaka in the forest of Naimishara.

6. Chapter 1, Shloka 3
   तम आश्रमम अनुप्राप्तं नैमिषारण्यवासिनः
   चित्रा: शरोतुं कथास तत्र परिववुस तपस्विनः

When he reached the dark hermitage, the inhabitants of the forest of Naimishara told him about the wonderful stories of the ascetics.

7. Chapter 1, Shloka 4

   अभिवाद्य मुनींस्तांस तु सर्वान एव कृताञ्जलिः
   अपृच्छत स तपोवृद्धिं सन्दिश चैवाभिनन्दितः

   Having saluted the sages, he inquired of them all with folded hands about the progress of their austerities and was greeted by the sages.

8. Chapter 1, Shloka 8 and 9

   जनमेजयस्य राजर्षेः सर्पसत्रे महात्मनः
   समीपे पार्थिवेन्द्रस्य सम्यक पारिक्षितस्य च
   कृष्णद्वैपायन परोक्ताः सुपुण्या विविधाः कथाः
   कथिताश चापि विधिवद या वैशम्पायनेन वै

   In the serpent sacrifice of the Rajarishi Janamejaya, in the presence of the great soul, the king of the earth, the son of Parikshit, Krishna Dwaipayana told various pious stories and they were told according to the rituals by Vaishampayana.

9. Chapter 1, Shloka 17

   भारतस्येतिहासस्य पुण्यां ग्रन्थार्थ संयुताम
   संस्कारोपगतां बराह्मीं नानाशास्त्रोपबृंहिताम

10. Chapter 1, Shloka 18

    जनमेजयस्य यां राज्ञो वैशम्पायन उक्तवान
    यथावत स ऋषिस तुष्ट्या सत्रे दवैपायनाज्ञया

11. Chapter 1, Shloka 19

    वेदैश चतुर्भिः समितां व्यासस्यादृत कर्मणः
    संहितां शरोतुम इच्छामो धर्म्यां पापभयापहाम

    Translation: Chapter 1, Shloka 17-19:
    We wish to read the sacred Brahmanical text of the history of India, the ritualized Brahman, enriched with various scriptures, which was spoken by Sage Vaishampayana in the sacrifice to the satisfaction of the King (Janamejaya).

12. Chapter 1, Shloka 61

    चतुर्विंशतिसाहस्रीं चक्रे भारत संहिताम
    उपाख्यानैर विना तावद भारतं परोच्यते बुधैः

    The twenty four thousand verses of the Bharata Samhita is so far described by the wise (Sage Vaishampayana) without the narratives.

BACKGROUND

*T*he Mahabharata epic originally composed by Sage Krishna Dwaipayana or Ved Vyasa was called Jaya or Bharata and was of 24,000 verses.

It was originally taught by Sage Krishna Dwaipayana to his son Suka and his disciple Vaishampayana.

King Parikshit, son of Abhimanyu, successor of the Pandavas to the Kuru Kingdom's throne has been mentioned in the epic to have been killed by Naga Takshaka, king of an exotic serpent race called 'Nagas' which seems to have co-existed with humans during the Mahabharata period.

The serpent race Nagas, as they are called finds mention in the epic prominently especially in the Khandava Daha Upa Parva or chapters of the Adi Parva which deals with displacement of this race from Khandava forest or vana which was burnt down by Arjuna, one of the five Pandava brothers, to make way for establishing a new kingdom in its place, which later came to be known as Indraprastha and corresponded to modern day Delhi, west of river Yamuna. The royal palace, assembly hall and other structures built in its aftermath, details of which has been mentioned in the Sabha parva of the epic and in Indraprastha chapter of this book, at least attests to building of a new township in this area.

The Nagas after getting displaced from their homeland where they had been dwelling, settled in and around Takshashila, or modern day Taxila in kingdom of Gandhara. The name of their abode 'Takshashila' itself might have been derived from name of the serpent king 'Takshaka'.

King Janamejaya, son of King Parikshit after ascending to throne and after knowing the story of his father's death, set out for Takshashila with his army, subdued the country, established it under his control and most importantly massacred and exterminated the race of Nagas with the exception of its King Takshaka. The Sarpa-Satra or serpent sacrifice ritual mentioned in the epic indicates towards the same.

The Mahabharata epic was recited by Sage Vaishampayana at behest of his Guru Sage Krishna Dwaipayana to King Janamejaya and other rishis and learned men probably at Takshashila itself. Amongst the audience was one professional storyteller or bard named Ugrasravas Sauti, who later retold the epic to a group of sages who had gathered at Naimishara or Naimisaranya forest (which corresponds to modern day Nimsar, situated along Gomati river in the Sitapur district of U.P.) during the reign of either King Satanika I (son of Janamejaya) or his son King Aswamedhadatta.

However, the Mahabharata epic recited by Ugrasravas Sauti is of 1,00,000 verses which got orally codified to its current form over a period of time by getting transmitted to successive generations orally till it was put down to writing in 2nd century B.C. or may be even earlier in Sanskrit Brahmi script.

The two major ancient Greek poems Iliad and Odyssey believed to be composed by Homer sometime in 8th or 7th century B.C. were also passed on in a similar fashion to successive generations' i.e. through oral tradition – ballads and performances by professional reciters of Homer known as 'Rhapsodes', put down to writing at end of the dark ages of Greek civilization, probably in early 5th century B.C. during time of ancient Greek historian Herodotus.

Greek writer and historian Dio Chrysostom (40-115 A.D.), mentions in his writings or orations that the Indians possess an Iliad of 1,00,000 verses.

One of the copper plate inscriptions (see image below) found in Khoh, Satna district, M.P., belongs to 6th century A.D. Probably a village grant, it mentions King Sharvanatha of Uchchhakalpa dynasty, who is believed to have ruled between 508-533 A.D. in that region.

That inscription describes Mahabharata as a collection of 1,00,000 verses.

Background

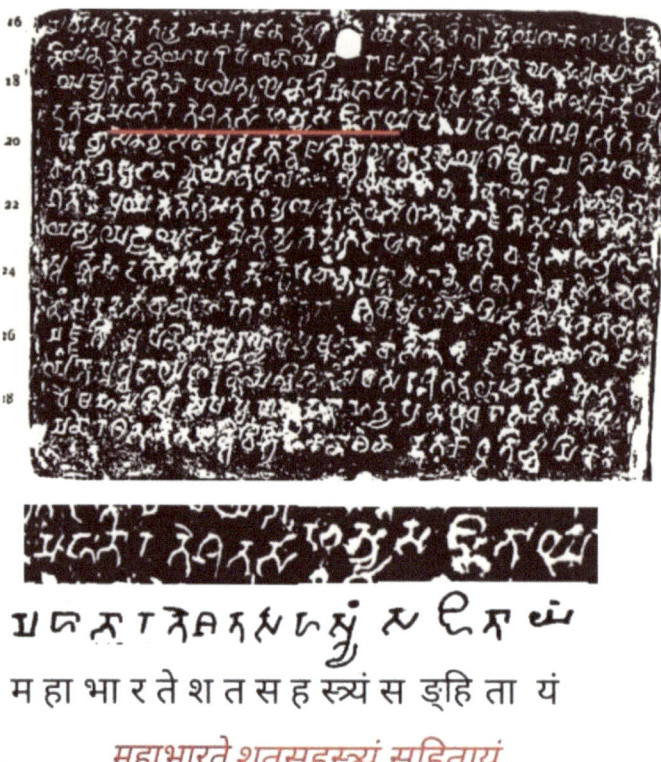

The entire Mahabharata epic of 1,00,000 verses is structured as a dialogue between Ugrasravas Sauti (the narrator) and Sage Saunaka (the narratee). The Bharata or Jaya of 24,000 verses recited by Sage Vaishampayana and composed by his Guru Sage Krishna Dwaipayana is embedded within these 1,00,000 verses.

We can conclude that the Mahabharata epic coded by Ugrasravas Sauti within 100 years of happening of the war was of 1,00,000 verses, not 24,000.

The earliest reference of Mahabharata comes from the ancient Sanskrit grammarian Panini in his work 'Ashtadhyayi' written in 4th century B.C. in Sanskrit Brahmi script during the reign of King Dhanananda of the Nanda dynasty of Magadha kingdom.

Ashtadhyayi verse 6.2.38:

महान् (प्रथमा-एकवचनम्) , व्रीहि-अपराह्ण-गृष्टि-इष्वास-जाबाल-भार-भारत-हैलिहिल-रौरव-प्रवृद्धेषु

काशिका :

प्रकृत्या पूर्वपदमिति वर्तते, द्वन्द्व इति निवृत्तम्। महानित्येतत् पूर्वपदं व्रीहि अपराह्ण गृष्टि इष्वास जाबाल भार भारत हैलिहिल रौरव प्रवृद्ध इत्येतेषूत्तरपदेषु प्रकृतिस्वरं भवति। महाव्रीहिः। महापराह्णः। महागृष्टिः। महेष्वांसः। महाजाबालः। महाभारः। महाभारतः। महाहैलिहिलः। महारौरवः। महाप्रवृद्धः। महच्छब्दोऽन्तोदात्तः। तस्य प्रतिपदोक्तो यः समासः सन्महत्परमोत्तमोत्कृष्टाः० २.१.६१ इति तत्रैव स्वरः। तेनैषां षष्ठीसमासोऽन्तोदात्त एव भवति — महतो व्रीहिः महद्व्रीहिरिति। कर्मधारयेऽनिष्ठा ६.२.४६ इत्ययमपि श्रेण्यादिसमासे २.१.५९ विधिरिति प्रवृद्धशब्द इह पठ्यते॥

Translation:
The word महत् (महा) retains its accent before the following - १. व्रीहि २. अपराह्ण ३. गृष्टि ४. इष्वास ५. जाबाल ६. भार ७. भारत ८. हैलिहिल ९. रौरव and १०. प्रवृद्धे।

Thus महाव्रीहिः; महापराह्णः; महागृष्टिः; महेष्वास; महाजाबाल; महाभार; महाभारत; महाहैलहिल; महारौरव; महाप्रवृद्धः ॥ The महत् has acute on the final. (Unadi II.८४) On the प्रतिपदोक्त maxim already mentioned under ६.२.२६, this accent will apply to that compound of महत् which it forms under rule २.१.६१, for that is the particular rule of Karmadharaya compounding relating to mahat (pratipadokta). This rule therefore, will not apply to Genitive Tatpurusha. Thus महतो व्रीहिः= महद्व्रीहिः which has accent on the final by ६.१.२२३.

Q. The word प्रवृद्ध is a Participle formed by क्त affix, and by rule ६.२.४६, in a Karmadharaya compound, the first member will retain its original accent. What is then the necessity of reading this word in this sutra? Ans. That sutra ६.२.४६ applies, on the maxim of pradipadokta, to the special participles and nouns mentioned in २.१.५९ and not to every participle and noun.

PART I

THE PURANAS AND THE AVERAGE REIGN PER RULER HYPOTHESIS

CHAPTER 1

THE EARLIEST BUDDHIST SHRINE: EXCAVATING THE BIRTH PLACE OF THE BUDDHA, LUMBINI (NEPAL) – R.A.E. CONINGHAM, K.P. ACHARY AND OTHERS

Excerpts from The Earliest Buddhist Shrine: Excavating the birth place of the Buddha, Lumbini (Nepal)

– R.A.E. Coningham,
K.P. Achary and others, 2013:

The cleaning of the sections left by the JBF in trenches C5, C7, C13 and ENE exposed

in situ cultural horizons beneath the Asokan walls, confirming Acharya's hypothesis that earlier activity pre-dated the 'Mauryan Horizon'. Indeed, OSL measurements from early land surfaces, contexts 508 and 509, within Trench C5 yielded dates of 545+-235 BC, and 990+-290 BC respectively. In addition, a radiocarbon date of 788–522 BC was obtained from context 561, another early cultural layer in Trench C5b (see Tables 1 & 2). Furthermore, ceramics recovered from the earliest cultural deposits included Cord Impressed Ware, which is found within regional Iron Age ceramic assemblages (Singh 1994: 107; Verardi 2007: 245–49). During the excavations, we were also able to distinguish the presence of at least two construction phases within the Asokan temple and roof tiles and lime plaster in contexts associated with its levelling. Our activities, however, were mainly focused in the centre of the temple in Trench C5. This represented the largest area of unexcavated material because the JBF had halted their work when they encountered "two rows of bricks" (Uesaka 2001: 51). When the surface of C5 was cleaned in 2012, we exposed an irregular brick pavement defined by an east–west kerb (Figure 7). This kerb was found to comprise large bricks measuring a maximum 520 × 380 × 75mm, weighing 19kg each, and marked with finger grooves on one surface. Once the brick pavement had been planned and removed, two earlier phases were identified and it was clear that the kerb had defined the edge of three successive pavements. Not only did these pavements run underneath the Asokan walls, the kerb itself was incorporated into the foundations of the Asokan temple, confirming that it was part of a pre-Asokan brick structure. As the lowermost pavement and kerb were removed, a series of six postholes following the same east–west alignment were exposed in the deposit below (Figure 8). This was highly significant: the kerb had replaced a line of wooden posts that had previously defined this space. Not only was there evidence of permanent constructions older than the Asokan temple but the presence of non-durable architecture had also been identified. Radiocarbon samples from two contemporary posthole fills (contexts 553 and 557) provided dates of 799–546 BC and 801–548 BC (Table 1), suggesting an extremely early delineation of sacred space within this locality, and pushing activity at Lumbini far before the reign of Asoka.

Table 1. Radiocarbon determinations from Trench C5b within the Maya Devi Temple.

Lab code	Sample	Site	Trench	Context	^{14}C age BP	Calibrated 68.2% (1σ)	Calibrated 95.4% (2σ)
SUERC-42856 (GU28693)	X70	MDT	C5b	553 (posthole fill)	2540±30	793–751 BC (34.7%) 687–667 BC (15.4%) 637–622 BC (7.1%) 615–594 BC (11.0%)	799–734 BC (39.4%) 691–662 BC (17.7%) 650–546 BC (38.2%)
(GU28694)	X71	MDT	C5b	555	Failed		
SUERC-42857 (GU28695)	X72	MDT	C5b	557 (posthole fill)	2548±30	796–752 BC (41.6%) 686–667 BC (15.0%) 633–625 BC (3.4%) 613–596 BC (8.2%)	801–741 BC (46.4%) 690–663 BC (17.4%) 648–548 BC (31.6%)
SUERC-42861 (GU28696)	X85	MDT	C5b	561 (early cultural layer)	2505±30	766–745 BC (10.5%) 688–664 BC (10.4%) 647–551 BC (47.2%)	788–522 BC (95.4%)
SUERC-42862 (GU28697)	X90	MDT	C5b	562 (natural soil)	3315±30	1627–1601 BC (20.4%) 1593–1532 BC (47.8%)	1681–1521 BC (95.4%)

Note: the sampling was undertaken in January 2012, and submitted for dating at the AMS Facility at the Scottish Universities Environmental Research Centre. The ^{14}C age is quoted in conventional years BP (before 1950 AD). The calibrated age ranges are determined from the University of Oxford Radiocarbon Accelerator Unit calibration program (OxCal3) (Bronk Ramsey 1995, 2001).

CHAPTER 2

THE AGE OF MAHAJANAPADAS
(FROM 623 B.C. TO 323 B.C.)

There were 16 great kingdoms and republics that had developed by late 7th century B.C. and flourished in a belt that stretched from current day Peshawar-Taxila to Bihar and upto Vindhyas down under. Their names are mentioned in Anguttara Nikaya (a Buddhist text). All of them were flourishing even before birth of Lord Buddha in 623 B.C. Prominent among them were Avanti, Vatsa and Magadha which we will be discussing in this chapter. The following map mentions names and shows location of all 16 mahajanapadas:

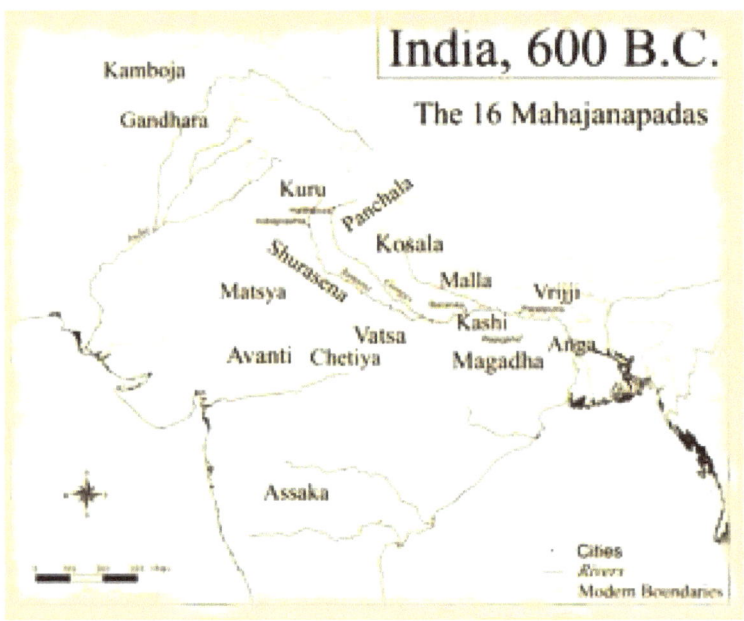

The birth of Lord Buddha happened in 623 B.C. as per Nepali tradition and the archaeological excavations at Maya Devi temple, Lumbini, (exact place of Lord Buddha's birth) mentioned in detail in previous chapter which shows a pre Mauryan era timber temple unearthed at that place, testing of which gives it a period of 799 B.C. to 546 B.C. or 801 B.C. to 548 B.C.

Translation of Brahmi inscription in Pali language on the Ashokan pillar discovered in year 1896 at Lumbini, Nepal called Rummindei pillar:

"When King Devanampriya Priyadarsin had been anointed twenty years, he came himself and worshipped (this spot) because the Buddha Shakyamuni was born here. (He) both caused to be made a stone bearing a horse (?) and caused a stone pillar to be set up, (in order to show) that the Blessed one was born here. (He) made the village of Lumbini free of taxes, and paying only an eighth share (of the produce).

Image of inscription on the Rummindei Ashokan Pillar at Lumbini (above).

This proves that Lord Buddha was born in Lumbini, Nepal and supports the 623 B.C. as his year of birth. Modern historians have erroneously put year of Lord Buddha's birth at 563 B.C. based upon the following information:

"The Buddha was born 298 years before Ashoka's coronation and died 218 years before the coronation."

– **Long Chronology of Mahavamsa.**

Ashoka's coronation happened around 269 B.C. – 265 B.C.

Haryanka Dynasty of Magadha Mahajanapada [As per Mahavamsa]			
S.No.	Name of the Ruler	Period of reign	No. of years of reign
1.	Bimbisara	602 – 550 B.C.	52
2.	Ajatashatru	550 – 519 B.C.	31
3.	Udayin or Udaybhadra	519 – 503 B.C.	16

4.	Anirudda and his son Munda	503 – 496 B.C.	7
5.	Nagadasaka	496 – 472 B.C.	24
Total Years of Reign			**130**

Average years of reign per ruler = 130/6
= 21.67

King Bimbisara was anointed on Magadha mahajanapada's throne at 15 years of age by his father Bhattiya.

Pradyota Dynasty of Avanti Mahajanapada [As per Visarasreni of Merutunga]			
S.No.	Name of the Ruler	Period of reign	No. of years of reign
1.	Pradyota or Chandra Mahasena	550 – 527 B.C.	23
2.	Palaka	527 – 503 B.C.	24
3.	Visakhayupa	503 – 453 B.C.	50
4.	Ajaka or Aryaka	453 – 432 B.C.	21
5.	Nandivardhana or Avantivardhana	432 – 412 B.C.	20
Total Years of Reign			**138**

Average years of reign per ruler = 138/5
= 27.6

The Puranas also give 138 years of reign for Pradyota dynasty. The Puranas, Svapnavasavadatta and the Pratijna – Yaugandharayana attributed to Bhasa have described King Udayana of Vatsa mahajanapada as a scion of Bharata – kula dynasty.

Bharata – kula Dynasty of Vatsa Mahajanapada [From 588 B.C. till its end around 519 -503 B.C.]

1. Satanika Parantapa or Satanika II.
2. Queen Mrigavati [Satanika's wife and Vajji Confederation's head Chetaka's daughter who ruled as regent for some years when King Udayana was a minor].
3. King Udayana or Udena.
4. Vahinara / Ahinara.
5. Dandapani / Khandapani.
6. Niramitra.

7. Kshemaka.

As per Svetambara tradition of Jains, Lord Mahavira was born in 599 B.C. and lived for 72 years attaining nirvana at 527 B.C.

> *"King Palaka was anointed as king of Avanti in the same night in which Lord Mahavira attained Nirvana (i.e. 527 B.C.)."*
>
> — **Kalpasutra, a Jain text.**

> *"When Palaka became a king, Ajatashatru was ruler of Magadha."*
>
> — **Bhasa**

The above two quotes perfectly matches with dynasty lists given in previous page. King Palaka indeed ascended the throne in 527 B.C. when King Ajatashatru was ruling Magadha.

The presumption of Lord Mahavira being born in 540 B.C. happened because Lord Buddha's birth year was predated by 60 years from 623 B.C. to 563 B.C. So, Lord Mahavira's birth date along with Haryanka dynasty's, Pradyota dynasty's and Shishunaga dynasty's years of reign had to be pre dated accordingly. In doing so, modern historians have erroneously given a very short reign of 30 years for Nanda dynasty of Magadha which will be discussed in later part of this chapter.

King Udayana's story mentioned in Ekottara Agama Sutra

The story goes something like this. When Lord Buddha gained enlightenment at 35 years of age i.e. in 588 B.C., he went to 'Trayastrimsa or Heaven of thirty three gods' for few months to preach to his mother Maya Devi, who was there in that heaven after her death. Unable to bear his absence, King Udayana of Vatsa mahajanapada fell ill and instructed his men to make an image of Lord Buddha. Consequently, a five foot image of Lord Buddha was carved out of sandalwood and this contributed to his recovery. This Sutra regards this as first image of Lord Buddha ever made.

Interpretation

This story mentioned in Ekottara Agama Sutra became the most important source based upon which modern historians concluded that King Udayana was ruling Vatsa

1. In 588 B.C., year when Lord Buddha gained enlightenment and
2. During 6th and 9th year after enlightenment i.e. 582 B.C. and 579 B.C. when Lord Buddha visited Kaushambi.

King Udayana is depicted as a contemporary of King Pradyota in various ancient Sanskrit plays and texts like:

1. Svapnavasavadatta.
2. Pratijna – Yaugandharayana.
3. Kathasaritsagara.
4. Priyadarsika.
5. Dhammapada.

King Pradyota came to throne in 550 B.C. which gives more than 38 years of rule for King Udayana [588 – 550 B.C.] to be called his contemporary.

King Udayana also married King Pradyota's daughter Vasvadatta as per above mentioned texts after remaining in King Pradyota's captivity for some time, which is unlikely to have happened at an advanced age.

Even if the long reign of King Udayana from 588 B.C. is presumed true, there are numerous references in Jain texts like 'Chapter 8th of Mahavira Charitra in Trishashti Shalaka Purusha Charitra' composed by Hemachandra in 12th century A.D. which shows King Pradyota was already a ruler of Avanti mahajanapada, when Queen Mrigavati, mother of King Udayana was ruling Vatsa mahajanapada as a regent for her minor son after death of King Satanika Parantapa. If Queen Mrigavati was ruling Vatsa mahajanapada before 588 B.C. (year of Lord Buddha's enlightenment), then how it is possible for King Pradyota to be her contemporary, if he came to throne in 550 B.C. only.

Conclusion

1. King Udayana did make first image of Lord Buddha but in 543 B.C., soon after Lord Buddha's nirvana. He had come to rule by then.
2. The story of Lord Buddha going to heaven to preach his mother seems more mythical than historical.
3. Vatsa mahajanapada was being ruled by King Satanika Parantapa at time of Lord Buddha's enlightenment in 588 B.C., and upto 550 B.C., when King Pradyota ascended to throne in Avanti and attacked Kaushambi.
4. Queen Mrigavati may have acted as a regent for few years after 550 B.C., but before Lord Buddha's death in 543 B.C.

Sample the following quote from Vayu Purana which formed the basis for another wrong presumption by our modern historians:

"Ashta – trimsachchhatam bhavyah Pradyotah
pancha te sutah hatva tesham yasah kritsnam Sisunaga bhavishyati."

Translated as Sishunaga will destroy the prestige of Pradyotas and will be king.

Shishunaga Dynasty of Magadha			
S.No.	Name of the Ruler	Period of reign	No. of years of reign
1.	Shishunaga	472 – 454 B.C.	18
2.	Kalashok or Kakavarna	454 – 426 B.C.	28
3.	Nandivardhana and his son Mahanandin	426 – 412 B.C.	14
Total Years of Reign			**60**

Average years of reign per ruler = 60/4
= 15

Shishunaga was an Amatya / minister in King Nagadasaka's court and became king due to public uprising against the latter's unjust rule which ended the Haryanka dynasty and made Shishunaga the king.

Let us go through some information mentioned in various Buddhist and Jain texts.

1. As per the Vinaya Pali texts of Buddhists, First Buddhist Council was held near Rajagriha under King Ajatashatru's patronage in 543 B.C. i.e. soon after Lord Buddha's nirvana. Second Buddhist Council was held in Vaishali in 443 B.C. i.e. exactly 100 years after Lord Buddha's nirvana during King Kakavarna's reign.
2. "Ajatashatru in order to dissuade Pradyota from attacking Magadha, built a fortified city near Ganges river which came to be known as Pataliputra. Rajagriha was surrounded by five towering hills. Ajatashatru made it unbreachable by filling the gaps in the hills with stone walls."
   – **Majjhima Nikaya, a Buddhist text.**
3. "When King Udayin ascended the throne, Avanti was still counted as an enemy of Udayin."
   – **Parisishtiparvan, a Jain text.**
4. "Udaybhadra or Udayin had many a times defeated Palaka, the son and successor of Pradyota. Vatsa, with its capital at Kaushambi was now the

only formidable kingdom, apart from Avanti, but even Vatsa perished and Palaka grew in power after his conquest of Kaushambi."

— **Kathasaritsagara.**

With the independence of Vatsa gone, the rival kingdoms or mahajanapadas of Avanti and Magadha were now face to face with each other i.e. both mahajanapadas borders were now touching each other.

5. "While he (Udayin) was listening to the discourse of a teacher, with a novice, the latter fell upon him and killed him with his concealed dagger. It is stated that this assassin was engaged or hired by his political rival, Palaka, the king of Avanti."

— **The Avasyaka Sutra, a Jain text telling us how King Udayin was killed.**

6. "King Bimbisara sent his royal physician Jivaka to Avanti to treat King Pradyota, when the latter fell ill."

— **Mulasarvastivada.**

7. "The kingdom of Vatsa was already a part of Avanti during the reign of Palaka and a prince of royal family Maniprabha was the governor of Kaushambi."

— **Avashyaka Kathanaka, a Jain text.**

Interpretation

Since, King Palaka died in 503 B.C., his death would have happened after King Udayin's assassination in the same year.

We know from both Visasreni of Merutunga and the Puranas that the Pradyota dynasty lasted for 138 years.

1. If we presume King Shishunaga annexed Avanti Mahajanapada (based upon what is written in Vayu Purana) the year he came to power overthrowing the last ruler of Haryanka dynasty i.e. in 472 B.C., then Pradyota dynasty of Avanti mahajanapada should have started from 472 + 138 = 610 B.C. which means King Palaka's death happened in 563 B.C. i.e. before King Udayin of Magadha mahajanapada came to power in 519 B.C. If that is the case, then how did King Palaka fight numerous battles against King Udayin finally managing to have him assassinated as mentioned in above quotes?
2. Also, the above mentioned quote from Majjhima Nikaya regarding Ajatashatru fortifying Rajagriha fearing attack from King Pradyota shows both were contemporaries. If Avanti mahajanapada was annexed by King Shishunaga of Magadha mahajanapada, then it pushes back reign of King

Pradyota to 610 – 587 B.C. period whereas King Ajatashatru came to power only in 550 B.C. In that case how can both be contemporaries?

Conclusion

King Shishunaga annexing Avanti mahajanapada presumption (based on the Vayu Purana quote) is wrong.

Nanda Dynasty of Magadha mahajanapada [412 – 323 B.C.]

1. Mahapadma Nanda or Ugrasena Nanda
2. Dhana Nanda

The Jain texts such as Parishishtiparvan and Avashyaka Sutra mentions the Nanda king was son of a courtesan by a barber.

Roman historian Quintus Curtis Rufus (1st century A.D.) states that according to Porus, this barber became the former queen's paramour, thanks to his attractive looks, treacherously assassinated the then king, usurped the throne by pretending to act as a guardian for the then princes and later killed the princes. The Nanda king who was contemporary of Porus and Alexander (indicating Dhananada) was son of this barber.

The barber here is none other than Mahapadma Nanda of the Puranas whom the Mahavamsa refers to as Ugrasena.

1. As per Matsya Purana, he ruled for 88 years.
2. As per Vayu Purana, he ruled for 28 years.
3. As per Mahavamsa, the entire Nanda dynasty ruled for 22 years.

The Puranas describe him as Ekarat (sole sovereign) and Sarva – Kshatrantaka (destroyer of all Kshatriyas). The Kshatriyas said to have been exterminated by Mahapadma Nanda include:

1. Maithalas or Videhans.
2. Ikshvakus or Kosalans.
3. Kasheyas or Kashi.
4. Panchalas, Kuru, Shurasenas.
5. Kalingas and Ashmakas.
6. Finally, Haiheyas and Vitihotras meaning Avanti.

The Greek accounts by Diodorus Siculus and others name only one Nanda king – Agrammes or Xandrammes which may be corruption of the Sanskrit word 'Augrasainya' (literally son or descendant of Ugrasena). Roman

Historian Quintus Curtis Rufus also states that the Nanda rule spanned two generations only and the dynasty was overthrown by Sandrakottus or Chandragupta. The Greek accounts also state that Agrammes was the ruler of Gangaridai (the Ganges valley) and the Prasii. Megasthanese had stated that Pataliputra was located in the country of Prasii, so we can infer it to mean eastern part of the empire.

Chandragupta Maurya conquered Bharutkutccha or Bharuch, also known as Barygaza (with archaeological evidence supporting continuous habitation from advent of Mauryan era in 323 B.C. till Gupta period and beyond), an important ancient trading port without any mention of him conquering Avanti mahajanapada in any ancient texts.

Conclusion

It can be assumed that Avanti mahajanapada was annexed in 412 B.C. by Magadha mahajanapada when King Mahapadma Nanda came to power and when Pradyota dynasty of Avanti had completed 138 years of rule.

If we presume Lord Buddha's birth year as 563 B.C. based upon ancient Buddhist text Mahavamsa, Lord Mahavira's birth year as 540 B.C. and accordingly Haryanka dynasty's 130 year rule from 543 B.C. to 413 B.C., Pradyota dynasty's 138 years rule from 491 B.C. to 353 B.C, then King Mahapadma Nanda should have been in power by 353 B.C. as Pradyota dynasty's rule ends that year. The same Mahavamsa mentions 22 years rule for Nanda dynasty which ended in the year 323 B.C. In other words, as per Mahavamsa Mahapadma Nanda or Ugrasena Nanda came to power in 345 B.C.

Then how did he annex Avanti in 353 B.C.?

Long reign for Mahapadma Nanda cannot be given by shortening the reign of Shishunaga rulers for we know from Vinaya Pali Buddhist texts that the 'Second Buddhist Council' happened 100 years after Lord Buddha's nirvana i.e. in 443 B.C. during King Kalashok or Kakvarna's reign. There are many scholars and historians who have given various dates to King Mahapadma's coronation like 364 B.C., 382 B.C. etc. but given the battles he waged against numerous mahajanapadas and other kingdoms of that time, subjugating them and bringing a vast portion of North, Central and East India under his control, it indicates towards a much longer reign for him, which is why presuming Lord Buddha's birth year as 563 B.C., Lord

Mahavira's as 540 B.C. and then squeezing the entire Mahajanapada history from thereon till 323 B.C., simply does not add up and is wrong.

Conclusively, the archaeological evidences mentioned in Chapter 1 of this book validates 623 B.C. as year of Lord Buddha's birth and accordingly Mahajanapada period from 623 B.C. to 323 B.C.

CHAPTER 3

THE DATE OF MAHABHARATA WAR AS PER PURANAS

The Bharata – Kula dynasty as per Puranas [After Mahabharata war]

1. Arjuna, ruling along with other Pandavas with Yudhishtira, eldest of them as emperor.
2. Abhimanyu [Son of Arjuna who got killed in the Mahabharata war, because of which the rule passed from Pandavas to Parikshit directly. **Hence, 29 rulers ruled till Kshemaka**].
3. Parikshit.
4. Janamejaya.
5. Satanika I.
6. Aswamedhadatta [Puranas were compiled and Itihasa or Mahabharata retold during his reign]
7. Asima Krishna.
8. Nichakra [Shifted kingdom to Kaushambi after Hastinapura was flooded by river Ganges, thereby Vatsa mahajanapada was created].
9. Ushna.
10. Chitraratha.
11. Vrishnimat.
12. Sushana.
13. Sunitha.
14. Richa.
15. Nrichaksu.
16. Sukhihala.
17. Pariplava.
18. Sunaya.
19. Medhavin.
20. Nripanjaya.
21. Mridu.
22. Tigma.
23. Vrihadratha.

24. Vasudana.
25. Satanika Parantapa or Satanika II.
26. Udayana.
27. Ahinara or Vahinara.
28. Khandapani or Dandapani.
29. Niramitra.
30. Kshemaka.

We know from various ancient texts, quotes of which are mentioned in Chapter 2 of Part I of this book that:

1. Vatsa kingdom was annexed by King Palaka of Avanti and its last king Kshemaka presumably killed by him.
2. There is no mention of any battle between Magadha and Avanti mahajanapadas in any of the ancient texts when King Ajatashatru was in power in Magadha (550 – 519 B.C.).
3. It is to be noted that Magadha and Avanti kingdoms came face to face, their paths crossed i.e. their borders touched each other only after Avanti annexed Vatsa after which the battles between both kingdoms escalated.
4. There is mention of numerous battles between King Palaka of Avanti and King Udayin of Magadha after the latter came to power in 519 B.C., upon death of his father King Ajatashatru.

Based upon the above inferences, we can conclude that the Bharata – kula dynasty ended with King Kshemaka of Vatsa sometime between 519 B.C. to 503 B.C. 503 B.C. is the year when King Palaka died after assassination of King Udayin in the same year.

In absence of exact year for end of Bharata – kula dynasty, let us assume two dates from 519 B.C to 503 B.C. period i.e.

Case I End of the dynasty in 519 B.C.

Case II End of the dynasty in 509 B.C.

King Mahapadma Nanda came to power in 412 B.C. as mentioned in detail in Chapter 2 of Part I of this book.

I. So, gap between King Kshemaka's death and coronation of King Mahapadma Nanda would have been:

Case I End of the dynasty in 519 B.C.

= 519 B.C. - 412 B.C.

= 107 years.

Case II End of the dynasty in 509 B.C.

= 509 B.C. - 412 B.C.

= 97 years.

The Vishnu Purana gives a timeline of 1015 years from birth of King Parikshit till coronation of King Mahapadma Nanda. The Vayu Purana gives a timeline of 1050 years for the same period.

Number of rulers of Bharata – kula dynasty during this period = 29.

II. Total years of reign of Bharata – kula dynasty as per Vishnu Purana:

Case I End of the dynasty in 519 B.C.

= 1015 - 107

= 908 years.

Case II End of the dynasty in 509 B.C.

= 1015 - 97 years

= 918 years.

III. Average years of reign per ruler as per Vishnu Purana:

Case I End of the dynasty in 519 B.C.

= 908/29

= 31.31 years.

Case II End of the dynasty in 509 B.C.

= 918/29

= 31.65 years.

IV. Total years of reign of Bharata – kula dynasty as per Vayu Purana:

Case I End of the dynasty in 519 B.C.

= 1050 - 107

= 943 years.

Case II End of the dynasty in 509 B.C.

= 1050 - 97

= 953 years.

V. Average years of reign per ruler as per Vayu Purana:

Case I End of the dynasty in 519 B.C.

= 943/29

= 32.517 years.

Case II End of the dynasty in 509 B.C.
= 953/29
= 32.86 years.

In recorded history of India and elsewhere in the world, there has been no dynasty with a long rule of more than 300 years, having an average reign per ruler of 31 to 33 years or more. The 1015 or 1050 years time period given by the Puranas is too long to be considered accurate or believable.

King Parikshit was in mother Uttara's womb at time of the Mahabharata war. He must have born in the same or next year after the Mahabharata war.

The 'Date of Mahabharata War as per the Puranas' based upon the above calculations will be as follows:

As per Vishnu Purana
= Year of King Mahapadma Nanda's Coronation + 1015
= 412 + 1015
= **1427 B.C.**

As per Vayu Purana
= Year of King Mahapadma's coronation + 1050
= 412 + 1050
= **1462 B.C.**

The following are some of the dynasties which ruled in India, some during ancient and some during medieval periods, all having total years of reign of more than 300 years, but an average reign per ruler of less than 31 years:

1. The Sisodia Dynasty of Mewar Kingdom (1326 A.D. to 1842 A.D.)
    Total years of reign   = 516 years.
    Total number of rulers   = 28
    Average years of reign per ruler = 516 / 28
                                    = 18.428 years.
2. The Swargadeo Dynasty of Ahom Kingdom (1228 A.D. to 1822 A.D.)
    Total years of reign   = 594 - Interregnum period of 17 years
                                    = 577 years.
    Total number of rulers   = 39
    Average years of reign per ruler = 577 / 39
                                    = 14.79 years.

3. The Eastern Ganga Dynasty of Kalinga Kingdom (498 A.D. to 1434 A.D.)
   Total years of reign = 936 years.
   Total number of rulers = 37
   Average years of reign per ruler = 936 / 37
   = 25.29 years.

4. The Imperial Chola Dynasty of Chola Kingdom (848 A.D. to 1279 A.D.)
   Total years of reign = 431 - Interregnum period of 4 years
   = 427 years.
   Total number of rulers = 20
   Average years of reign per ruler = 427 / 20
   = 21.35 years.

5. Eastern Chalukyas or Chalukyas of Vengi Dynasty (624 A.D. to 1075 A.D.)
   Total years of reign = 451 - Interregnum period of 30 years
   = 421 years.
   Total number of rulers = 29
   Average years of reign per ruler = 421 / 29
   = 14.517 years.

6. The Pala Dynasty of Vanga (750 A.D. to 1165 A.D.)
   Total years of reign = 415 - Interregnum period of 6 years
   = 409 years.
   Total number of rulers = 21
   Average years of reign per ruler = 409 / 21
   = 19.47 years.

7. The Nala Dynasty of Dakshin Kalinga Kingdom (400 A.D. to 740 A.D.)
   Total years of reign = 340 - Interregnum period of 3 years
   = 337 years.
   Total number of rulers = 11
   Average years of reign per ruler = 337 / 11
   = 30.6 years.

8. Gurjara – Pratihara Dynasty of Rajputana Kingdom (730 A.D. to 1036 A.D.)
   Total years of reign = 306 years.
   Total number of rulers = 18
   Average years of reign per ruler = 306 / 18
   = 17 years.

Conclusion

Average years of reign per ruler varies between 14.517 years to 30.6 years in all the above mentioned 8 dynasties which has a 'total years of reign' of between 306 years to 936 years.

Average years of reign per ruler of more than 26 years is seen only once that is in case of Nala dynasty of Orissa (30.6 years). As evident from Eastern Ganga dynasty's extraordinary long rule of 936 years (which is part of our country's recorded history) such long reign is possible for a dynasty and that too with an average reign of around 25 to 26 years per ruler. But, when extent of territory ruled is huge and / or when ruled for extraordinarily long period say 400 years or more as evident from Eastern Chalukya dynasty, Pala dynasty and Sisodia dynasty, average reign per ruler does not go beyond **26.**

Since number of rulers in Bharata – kula dynasty from the conclusion of Mahabharata war till the dynasty's end was only 29, Mahabharata war must have happened well after the dates we arrive at as per Vishnu Purana and Vayu Purana.

Presuming an average reign of 26 years per ruler, number of years between conclusion of Mahabharata war and till Bharata – kula dynasty's end
= 29*26
= 754 years.
Case I End of the dynasty in 519 B.C.
Mahabharata war must have happened after
= 519 + 754
= **1273 B.C.**
Case II End of the dynasty in 509 B.C.
Mahabharata war must have happened after
= 509 + 754
= **1263 B.C.**

CHAPTER 4

APPROXIMATE DATING OF MAHABHARATA WAR

Brihadratha Dynasty of Magadha Kingdom

The Mahabharata states that King Jarasandha was son of King Brihadratha, founder of the Brihadratha dynasty of Magadha. The ancient text also states that King Jarasandha's son Sahadeva was killed in the great war at Kurukshetra. As per Vayu Purana, a total of 21 kings from this dynasty ruled Magadha since the conclusion of the Mahabharata war for around 1000 years.

The following is the list of rulers mentioned therein:

1. Somadhi.
2. Srutasravas.
3. Ayutayus.
4. Niramitra.
5. Sukshatra.
6. Brihatkarman.
7. Senajit.
8. Srutanjaya.
9. Vipra.
10. Suchi.
11. Kshemya.
12. Subrata.
13. Dharma.
14. Susuma.
15. Dridhasena.
16. Sumati.
17. Subala.
18. Sunita.
19. Satyajit.
20. Viswajit.
21. Ripunjaya.

As per Vayu Purana, the last ruler of this dynasty was killed by his minister Pulika, who then started the Pradyota dynasty by enthroning his son Pradyota and that this dynasty then ruled Magadha kingdom for next 138 years. It has been conclusively established in this book's 'Age of Mahajanapadas' chapter as well as by historians through ancient Buddhist and Jain texts that Pradyota dynasty ruled Avanti mahajanapada not Magadha and was a contemporary of Haryanka dynasty of Magadha i.e. both were co-existing.

Secondly, with 21 rulers, Brihadratha dynasty could have hardly continued for maximum 546 years presuming an average reign of 26 years per ruler. Total reign of 1000 years is impossible. But, we can infer from the Vayu Purana that the dynasty must have indeed ruled for a very long time and thus average years of reign per ruler would be high.

The Haryanka dynasty of Magadha started with King Bimbisara ascending the throne in 602 B.C., at age of 15 years is something which we conclude based upon writings in ancient texts such as Mahavamsa. Lord Buddha's and Lord Mahavira's year of birth is taken as 623 B.C. and 599 B.C. respectively as per the respective religion's traditional beliefs, supported by evidences mentioned in previous chapters.

No ancient Buddhist or Jain text mentions King Bimbisara's father Bhattiya as King of Magadha or first king or founder of the Haryanka dynasty nor there is mention of any early rulers of Magadha, puranic or otherwise preceding the Haryanka dynasty, nor is there any mention of Magadha Kingdom itself before coming of King Bimbisara and his father.

The Vidhura Pandita Jataka describes Rajagriha (Magadhan capital) as the city of Anga kingdom. According to Kathasaritsagara, the Angeya city of Vitankapura was located on shores of the sea (which indicates extent of Anga kingdom's boundaries was upto Bay of Bengal sea). The Mahavamsa mentions father of King Bimbisara i.e. Bhattiya was defeated by King Brahmadatta of Anga. This defeat was later avenged by King Bimbisara who annexed Anga during later part of his rule and appointed his son Kunika or Ajatashatru as its governor or ruler.

This proves that Anga was an independent kingdom during King Brahmadatta's reign till it got annexed by Magadha.

According to the Puranic accounts, the Vitihotras, one of the five Haiheya clans were ruling Avanti kingdom including its two capitals Ujjaini and Mahishmati. It is most likely that Pulika, an amatya/minister must have overthrown the last Vitihotra ruler to place his son Pradyota on the throne.

The Jatakas tell us that King Bimbisara married Kosala Devi, daughter of King Sanjaya Mahakosala of Kosala kingdom and got a village in Kasi, yielding a revenue of a hundred thousand for bath and perfume money (i.e. as dowry). This along with mention in Jatakas of King Kamsa or Baranasiggaha of Kosala kingdom ruling Kasi proves beyond doubt that Kasi had come under Kosala kingdoms's rule a few years before Sanjaya Mahakosala came to power and thus ceased to be an independent kingdom.

The Mahagovindasuttanta of the Dighanikaya

This ancient Buddhist text corresponds to pre – Pradyota and pre – Haryanka dynasty period. Avanti including its city Mahishmati is mentioned in it as being ruled by King Vessabhu or Vishvabhu. From what is mentioned in the Puranas, we can infer that he was a Vitihotra ruler and was ruling Avanti before 550 B.C.

A certain king Brahmadatta of Kasi has been mentioned in the Mahagovindasuttanta as holding suzerainty over Assaka or Asmaka kingdom of Deccan and its capital Potali, indicating he was ruler of an independent and powerful Kasi kingdom.

> "Sattabhu, Brahmadatta, Vessabhu and Bharata, Renu and two Dhataratthas, these are seven Bharat kings."
>
> – As per The Mahagovindasuttanta of the Dighanikaya.

It mentions Anga kingdom ruled by King Dhatarattha.
In the Mahagovindasuttanta of the Dighanikaya,

1. There is no mention of any of the 21 kings of the Vayu Purana's list of Brihadratha dynasty rulers.
2. There is no mention of Magadha kingdom or any of its rulers ruling the region predating King Bimbisara's reign.
3. There is no mention of conquest of Magadha region or territory by King Dhatarattha of Anga.

Based upon the above observations, we can conclude that King Bimbisara's father Bhattiya captured back Rajagriha from King Brahmadatta of Anga in 602 B.C. and anointed his son as King of the revived Magadha kingdom, thereby starting the Haryanka dynasty.

"At time of King Prasenjit's death, the Kosala king was eighty years of age, the same age as Lord Buddha."

**– Majjhima Pannasa Pali,
Dhammacetiya Sutta.**

Lord Buddha died in 543 B.C., at 80 years of age which means so did King Prasenjit of Kosala, after Vidudabha, son of King Prasenjit usurped the Kosala throne from him the same year. This means King Prasenjit of Kosala was also born in 623 B.C., the year of Lord Buddha's birth. In other words, King Sanjaya Mahakosala, father of King Prasenjit was ruling Kosala kingdom in 623 B.C.

Kasi kingdom was annexed by one of King Sanjaya Mahakosala's predecessor King Kamsa as per the Jatakas. This means Kasi kingdom was an independent kingdom till sometime before Lord Buddha's birth in 623 B.C.

The Mahagovindasuttanta of the Dighanikaya is an ancient Buddhist text because of which it is unlikely to describe events which happened in Late Vedic Age i.e. before 700 B.C. and upto 900 B.C.

Moreover, Anguttara Nikaya, another Buddhist text mentions Kasi as one of the 16 mahajanapadas of Bharatavarsha. The same text mentions Magadha as another mahajanapada. The text could not have corresponded to King Bimbisara's reign as Kasi was no longer an independent kingdom during his reign and before that Magadha was a part of Anga kingdom.

We can put the date at around 650 B.C. when both Magadha and Kasi mahajanapadas co-existed, were independent and hence finds mention in the Anguttara Nikaya as part of the 16 mahajanapadas of Bharatavarsha that co-existed at that time.

King Brahmadatta of the Mahagovindasuttanta must have been ruler of the independent Kasi kingdom around 640 B.C., shortly after which it might have become part of Kosala kingdom. King Dhatarattha of Anga has been mentioned along with King Brahmadatta of Kasi in that text i.e. both were contemporaries.

As already mentioned in this chapter, there is no mention of conquest of the Magadha region by King Dhatarattha of Anga nor there is any mention of Magadha in the Mahagovindasuttanta of the Dighanikaya. No early rulers of Magadha, puranic or other wise preceding King Bimbisara and his father Bhattiya have been mentioned in any of the ancient Buddhist and Jain texts.

Conclusion

We can thus conclude that the Brihadratha dynasty's rule of Magadha kingdom must have ended with conquest of Magadha kingdom by Anga kingdom during reign of one of King Dhatarattha's predecessors probably around 650 B.C. This dynasty as told earlier must not have ruled for more than 546 years (presuming an average reign of 26 years per ruler).

This means Mahabharata war must have happened sometime after:

= 650 + 546
= 1196 B.C.

PART II

MAHABHARATA EPIC, A HISTORICAL ACCOUNT NOT MYTHOLOGICAL

CHAPTER 1

THE BRAHMI SCRIPT

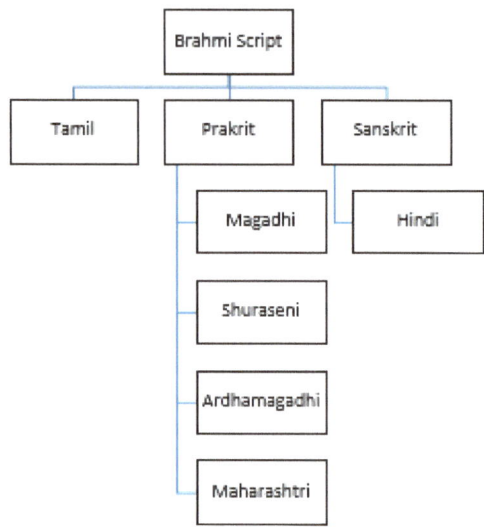

The Ashokan Pillar edicts were earliest literary / written evidence of Prakrit Brahmi, the first form of writing that developed in Bharatavarsha. It could not have been developed before 261 B.C. i.e. Year of Magadh – Kalinga war. That's when King Ashoka is believed to have given up further military conquests seeing the bloodshed in the Kalinga war. As per one of his rock edict inscriptions, 1 lakh people died in the war and 1.5 lakhs taken captive. From thereon, he started focusing on arts, culture, religion etc. and development of system of writing seems to be the result of this newly found pursuit.

Bhattiporulu and Mangulam inscriptions both date to late 3rd century B.C. While the former is written in Prakrit Brahmi and old telegu language, the latter is earliest Tamil Brahmi inscription and mentions that workers of Nedunchezhiyan I, a Sangam age Pandyan King made stone beds for Jain monks. It gives names of the workers and for whom the beds were made. Tamil Brahmi evolved later than Prakrit Brahmi i.e. the script evolved from North to South India, not the other way round as many people believe it to be. Gandhari Prakrit was a language written in Kharosthi script as evident from 'Gandharan Buddhist texts' of 1st century A.D.

Sanskrit Language in Brahmi Script

From the time of composition of Rig Veda, somewhere before 1800 B.C. or before advent of Iron Age in India till end of Mahajanapada period in 323 B.C., oral composition of Hindu religion's sacred texts and subsequent transmission from one generation to another through oral tradition had been prevalent social practice or custom. The sacred texts that were orally composed during this time were:

1. The Four Vedas i.e. Rig Veda, Sama Veda, Yajur Veda and Atharva Veda.
2. Bhagvata Purana or Srimad Bhagvatam.
3. Manusmriti.
4. Mahabharata.
5. Vayu Purana, Matsya Purana, Vishnu Purana etc.
6. Shatapatha Brahmana and Aitareya Brahmana
7. Upanishads

Six Vedangas (limbs of Vedas) were evolved for the proper understanding of the Vedas, namely:

1. Siksha (Phonetics)
2. Kalpa (Rituals)
3. Vyakarna (Grammar)
4. Nirukta (Etymology)
5. Chhanda (Metrics)
6. Jyotisha (Astronomy)

The third aspect i.e. Vyakarna (Grammar) of Sanskrit is 'Ashtadhyayi', a grammatical treatise that essentially lays the foundation of the Sanskrit language that we learn today. It consists of 3959 sutras in eight chapters which are divided into four sections or padas. It is supplemented by three ancillary texts:

1. The Akarasamamnaya
2. The Dhatupatha
3. The Ganapatha.

All have been composed by Panini which along with his predecessor Yaska's Nirukta was a result of centuries long effort to break the oral tradition of transmitting and teaching the sacred texts and to preserve Sanskrit language from corruption. Both Panini and Yaska were ancient Sanskrit grammarians and linguists, accepted by historians and scholars as historical figures. The Sanskrit epic Brihatkatha and the Buddhist scripture Manjusri-mula-kalpa, both mention Panini to have been a contemporary of King Dhanananda of the Nanda dynasty. Also, Panini's Rupya mentions a specific gold coin, the Niska in several sutras which was introduced in Bharatavarsha in the late 4th century B.C. and was a successor of Karshapanas, the earlier silver based coin.

It is highly unlikely that both Ashtadhyayi by Panini and Nirukta by Yaska would have been composed orally. Both had been put to writing in Sanskrit language and in Brahmi script and so had been other famous literary works of the time like the 'Arthashastra' and 'Chanakya Niti' by Acharya Chanakya or Kautilya, all of them in 4th century B.C.

This is where the Sanskrit Dilemma comes in.

As a language, Sanskrit is the oldest, older than Pali which in fact was derived from Sanskrit. During the Mahajanapada era (623 B.C. – 323 B.C.) Sanskrit was a language of the learned and scholars and the various Prakrit dialects and Pali (during Ashoka's reign) were language of the masses. But when it comes to evidence, the earliest Sanskrit inscriptions do not predate 2nd century B.C. Since the author does not have any substantial evidence to put forth for backing the claim that Sanskrit language was put to writing in Brahmi script in 4th century B.C., and that the Prakrit Brahmi and Tamil Brahmi evolved later, so in subsequent chapters Sanskrit Brahmi script has been mentioned to have evolved only in 2nd century B.C.

The following are the four earliest Sanskrit Brahmi inscriptions found in Bharatavarsha:

1. The Nasik Inscription of Ushavadata.
2. The Naneghat Inscriptions.
3. The Ayodhya Inscription of Dhana.
4. The Hathibada Ghosundi Inscriptions.

The Nasik Inscription of Ushavadata:

King Chastana of the Bhadramukhas or Kardamaka dynasty of the Western Kshatrapas ascended the Saka throne at beginning of the Saka era i.e. 78 A.D. King Nahapana, his predecessor is believed to have ruled for 5 years between 73 A.D. to 78 A.D. The Nasik inscription of Ushavadata reveals that King Nahapana's son-in law and Dinika's son Ushavadata built the Cave number 10 for Buddhist monks.

Nasik Cave inscription No.10. of Nahapana, Cave No.10

Translation:

"Success! Ushavadata, son of Dinika, son-in-law of King Nahapana, the Kshatrata, Kshatrapa (..) inspired by true religion in the Trirasami hills at Govardhana has caused this cave to be made and these cisterns."

Inscription No. 12 reads:

"Success! In the year 42, in the month of Vesakha, Ushavadata, son of Dinika, son-in-law of King Nahapana the Kshatrata Kshatrapa has bestowed this cave on the Sangha generally."

Saka era started in 78 A.D. So, "In the year 42" means the caves were built in

= 78 + 42
= 120 A.D.

The Naneghat Inscription:

The Naneghat Inscription are attributed to a queen of the Satavahana dynasty which means it is most likely to be written around 1st century A.D. or 2nd century A.D.

The Ayodhya Inscription of Dhana:

Shunga Dynasty of Magadha and Vidisha			
S.No.	Name of the Ruler	Period of reign	No. of years of reign
1.	Pushyamitra Shunga	185 B.C. – 149 B.C.	36
2.	Agnimitra Shunga	149 B.C. – 141 B.C.	8
3.	Vasujyeshtha Shunga	141 B.C. – 131 B.C.	10
4.	Vasumitra Shunga	131 B.C. – 114 B.C.	17
5.	Bhagabhadra or Bhadraka	114 B.C – 83 B.C.	31
6.	Devabhuti	83 B.C. – 73 B.C.	10
Total Years of Reign			**112**

Average years of reign per ruler = 112/6
= 18.67

The discovered inscription is damaged and incomplete. It reads:

1. Kosal – adhipena – dvir – asvamedha – yajinah senapateh Pushyamitrasya shashthena Kausiki – putrena Dhana.
2. Dharmarajna pituh Phalgudevasya ketanam karitam.

Translation:

"Dhana, Lord of Kosala, son of Kausiki, the sixth of the Senapati Pushyamitra, who had performed the Ashvamedha twice, erected a shrine (or other memorial) in honour of Phalgudeva, the father of the Dharmaraja."

The Vayu Purana and the Brahmanda Purana states seven powerful kings ruled in the capital of Kosala. Five Deva kings are attested by their coins namely Mula – deva, Vayu – deva, Vishakha – deva, Patha – deva and Dhana – deva. Another king Phalgu – deva, father of Dhana – deva is attested by this Ayodhya inscription. In 7th century A.D. text Harshacharitra, a king Mitradeva is mentioned to have killed Sumitra or Vasumitra, the Shunga king and son of Agnimitra. The text also mentions King Muladeva's name.

Based upon this, we can infer the chronology to be:

Deva Dynasty of Saketa:

1. Muladeva (vassal of Pushyamitra Shunga).
2. Mitradeva (killed Vasumitra Shunga in 114 B.C.).

3. 3rd 4th and 7th : Kings Vayudeva, Pathadeva and Vishakhadeva [It is not known who was the 3rd, 4th and 7th ruler.
4. 5th ruler: Phalgudeva and 6th ruler: Dhanadeva.

Dhanadeva has been mentioned in the Ayodhya inscription as sixth of the dynasty which started at the time of Pushyamitra Shunga.

The Yuga Purana is a Sanskrit text and part of Vriddhagargiya Samhita, an astrology text. It is described in style of prophecy (future tense) probably compiled and written sometime around 25 B.C. after end of Indo Greek kingdom of Taxila and Sakala. The Yuga Purana initially mentions Saketa as the residence of a governor which possibly could have been King Muladeva of this Deva dynasty.

Later it describes Saketa or Ayodhya being attacked by Yavanas (Greeks). This is also attested by Mahabhashya of Patanjali which mentions siege of Saketa and Mathura by Yavanas under Meneander I. The Yuga Purana also states that Saketa was ruled by seven powerful kings after retreat of the Yavanas.

> *"Those who came after Alexander went to the Ganges and Pataliputra."*
>
> **– Strabo, greek historian.**

> *"After having conquered Saketa, the country of the Panchala and the Mathuras, the Yavanas (Greeks), wicked and valiant, will reach Kusumadhvaja. The thick mud – fortifications at Pataliputra being reached, all the provinces will be in disorder, without a doubt. Ultimately a great battle will follow with tree like engines (siege engines)."*
>
> **– Gargi Samhita, Yuga Purana, Ch – 5.**

The Yavana retreat from Saketa must have happened only after the death of King Meneander I in 130 B.C. after which the Deva dynasty under King Mularaja declared themselves sovereign. If King Mitradeva was ruling Saketa in 114 B.C. at time of King Vasumitra of Shunga dynasty's death, then the reign of King Dhanadeva and his Ayodhya inscription cannot predate 50 B.C.

The Hathibada Ghosundi Inscriptions:

This is the oldest Sanskrit Inscriptions in Brahmi script and dated to 2nd century B.C. It is found near Nagari village (Hathibada), about 13 km north of Chittorgarh, Rajasthan and Ghosundi village, about 4.8 km southwest of Chittorgarh, Rajasthan. A part of the inscription read as:

1. Karito = yam rajna Bhagava tena Gajayanena Parasariputrena Sa –
2. Rvatatena Asvamedhayajjna bhagava bhyaih Samkarshana – Vasudevabhyam.
3. Anihatabhyrah sarvesvara bhyam pujasila – prakaro Narayana – vatika.
   D.R. Bhandarkar, Archaeologist.

> Translation by D.R. Bhandarkar, an archaeologist
> "(This) enclosing wall round the stone (object) of worship called Narayana – vatika (compound) for the divinities Samkarshana – Vasudeva who are unconquered and lords of all (has been caused to be made) by (the king) Sarvatata, a Gajayana and son of (a lady) of the Parasaragotra who is devotee of Bhagvat (Vasudeva or Samkarshana) and has performed an Ashvamedha sacrifice."

The text refers to a temple of Lord Krishna and Lord Balarama which was built by or during reign of a King Sarvatata who had performed an Ashvamedha sacrifice.

For the unversed, let us explain what an Ashvamedha sacrifice is:

It is a horse sacrifice ritual followed by ancient Hindu kings to prove their imperial sovereignty; a horse accompanied by the king's warriors or soldiers would be released to wander for a long duration traversing territories of rival kings in Bharatavarsha. Any rival king who do not wish to accept the Ashvamedha king's overlordship or suzerainty over his kingdom can fight the soldiers accompanying the horse. If the king performing the Ashvamedha yagya and his soldiers accompanying the horse remain undefeated during the period of traverse, the animal would be then guided back to the kingdom and sacrificed, and the king would then be declared Chakravartin or undisputed emperor of the land.

King Yudhishtira performed the Ashvamedha yagya in the Mahabharata after the great war at Kurukshetra, details of which is mentioned in the Aswamedha Parva of the epic where the sacrificial horse traverses to far off kingdoms like Sindh – Sauvira, Pragjyotisha (Assam) etc.

In short, for performing this ritual, the kingdom has to be militarily very strong i.e. strong enough to defeat any rival kingdom in the Indian subcontinent. Only one king had performed this horse sacrificing ritual (and that too twice during his reign) in recorded history of ancient India that is from Lord Buddha's birth in 623 B.C. till the end of Shunga dynasty in 73 B.C. The king is none other than Pushyamitra Shunga. Not only the Ayodhya inscription of Dhana, but also Malavika – agnimitram, a Sanskrit play composed by Kalidasa, the great poet attests to this fact.

"News is brought of the victory of Agnimitra's son Vasumitra who was employed by Agnimitra's father Pushyamitra Shunga to guard his sacrificial horse (which he did by defeating a cavalry squadron of the Yavanas on the banks of Indus River, probably near Sakala or Sialkot which was capital of Indo Greeks and the city in which Buddhist texts allege Pushyamitra committed atrocities against Buddhist monks after the victory). The Queen on knowing all these and her promise to reward Malavika gives her to the King (Agnimitra) and gladly consents to their union."

– **Act5, verse 14 of Malavika – Agnimitram by Kalidasa.**

The first Ashvamedha yagya was performed by King Pushyamitra Shunga soon after coming to throne by killing King Brahadattha, last ruler of the Mauryan dynasty in whose court he was the commander – in – chief of his army in 185 B.C.

Samkarshana or Lord Balarama and Vasudeva or Lord Krishna (above) on coins of Agathocles of Bactria who ruled from 190 – 180 B.C. or 185 to 180 B.C. from Taxila or Takshashila.

The Heliodorus pillar of Besnagar near Vidisha (capital of later Shunga rulers) which as per the inscription on it was erected in the 14th regnal year of King Bhagabhadra of Shunga dynasty which corresponds to 100 B.C. by Heliodorus, a Greek ambassador from the court of King Antialkidas of Indo Greek kingdom at Taxila.

Image of the Heliodorus Pillar and the main inscription on it (above).

The spread of Hinduism in general and Vaishnavism in particular was at its zenith or peak in entire Bharatavarsha during reign of the Shunga Dynasty. We can hence conclude that the King Sarvatata who had made the Krishna – Balarama temple or in whose reign the temple was constructed which as per the inscription is the one who had performed the Ashvamedha yagya is none other than King Pushyamitra Shunga and the Hathibada Ghosundi inscriptions dates back to sometime between 185 B.C. to 149 B.C., the 36 years of King Pushyamitra Shunga's reign.

It was during his rule that Patanjali, the revered scholar, composed Mahabhashya, another ancient treatise on Sanskrit grammar and linguistics, based upon his predecessor Panini's Ashtadhyayi. The Harshacharitra of Banabhatta records Pushyamitra Shunga's life and events during that time. He was a staunch follower of Hinduism, performed 'Rajasuiya yagya'[1] (tribute collection from rival kingdoms), did not patronize the Buddhist scholars and monks. As a result, the Buddhist texts have spewed venom against him, claiming him to be a persecutor of Buddhists and portraying his rule as usurping of Buddhist rule by Brahmins.

---

[1] *This yagya was also performed by the Pandavas declaring Yudhishtira as Chakravartin / Emperor after collecting tribute from more than 100 kings of Bharatavarsha or Indian subcontinent and killing King Jarasandha of Magadha kingdom, another contender for the Chakravartin title and performing of Rajasuiya yagya.*

Hinduism and Sanskrit language saw revival of some sorts during his dynasty's rule after being ignored for centuries by previous monarchs. The author believes given the space accorded to Hinduism in his dynasty's rule and dating of the Hathibada Ghosundi inscriptions to his reign (185 – 149 B.C.), not only Mahabhashya of Patanjali, but all the sacred Hindu texts mentioned in early part of this chapter including Mahabharata were put to writing in Sanskrit Brahmi script during the reign of King Pushyamitra Shunga.

Conclusion:

In other words, the Mahabharata epic was first written in Sanskrit Brahmi script (and not Prakrit Brahmi or Tamil Brahmi script) and was written sometime between 185 – 149 B.C. as the then dispensation was conducive for Sanskrit language and literature to thrive and prosper.

CHAPTER 2

THE WAR. WAR CHARIOTS AND WAR HORSES

I. Earliest literary references to Indian kingdoms in recorded ancient history – Behistun and other inscriptions

The Behistun Inscription:

It is a trilingual Achaemenid / Persian royal cuneiform inscription in a large rock relief on a cliff at Mount Behistun in Kermanshah province of Iran, near the city of Kermanshah, authored by King Darius I, sometime between 522 B.C., when he was coronated as King and 490 B.C., when first Persian invasion of Greece commenced. The inscription among other things mentions two kingdoms Gandhara and Sattagydia as a Kshatrapy or Satrapy i.e. tribute paying region and part of Achaemenid Empire under its King Darius I of Persia.

Gandhara, one of the 16 mahajanapadas mentioned in the ancient Buddhist text Anguttara Nikaya seems to have come under the sway or control of the Achaemenid Empire during the rule of King Darius I along with another kingdom Sattagydia, both of which as per Herodotus (one of earliest known historian in recorded ancient history) together with Dadicae (Daradas) and Aparytae formed the 7th province of Achaemenid Empire for tax and tribute payment purposes.

> *"The Sattagydae, Gandarii, Dadicae and Aparytae paid together a hundred and seventy talents; this was the seventh province."*
> **– Histories, Book III, Chapter 91 by Herodotus.**

Kshatrapas or Satraps as they were called were vassals or hyparch rulers in their own right, professing subjugation and allegiance to the empire and emperor by:

1. Regularly paying them the levied tribute and taxes.
2. Making available their army to them during military conquests and invasions.

In return they will be allowed to retain their independence.

The three kingdoms Sattagydia, Dadicae and Aparytae were located very near to or adjacent to Gandhara kingdom as all four have been mentioned together by Herodotus to form a province. The Daradas however are believed to have been inhabitants of Gilgit region of Kashmir and find mention in the Mahabharata epic. The Sattagydia kingdom, known in old Persian as Thatagus, country of the hundred cows is believed to have been situated in and around modern day Bannu city in Khyber Pakhtunwa, Pakistan and the kingdom of Aparytae was situated somewhere in between Sattagydia and Gandhara kingdoms. Archaeological evidences from Bannu and nearby places up to Peshawar are supportive of this viewpoint.

Some of the prominent ancient cities of Gandhara kingdom were:

1. Pushkalavati (Charsadda) – Capital of Gandhara kingdom.
2. Purushpura (Peshawar).
3. Taxila, ancient centre of learning.

Together, they were indeed crown jewel of Bharatavarsha.

King Ambhi was ruling Gandhara at time of Alexander the Great. He surrendered to Alexander and became his vassal. He took part in the Battle of Hydaspes with around 5000 men alongside Alexander, as per Greek accounts.

> *"King Darius says: These are the countries which are subject unto me, and by the grace of Ahuramazda I became king of them: Persia (Parsa), Elam (Uvja), Babylonia (Babirus), Assyria (Athura), Arabia (Arabaya), Egypt (Mudraya), the countries by the Sea, Lydia (Sparda), the Greeks (Yauna / Ionia), Media (Mada), Armenia (Armina), Cappadocia (Katpatuka), Parthia (Parthava), Drangiana (Zraka), Aria (Haraiva), Chorasmia (Uvarazmiy), Bactria (Baxtris), Sogdia (Suguda), Gandara (Gadara), Scythia (Saka), Sattagydia (Thatagus), Archosia (Harauvatis) and Maka (Maka); twenty – three lands in all."*
>
> **– Behistun Inscription of King Darius I.**

It mentions a total of 23 provinces as part of the Achaemenid Empire. However, another province called 'Hidus' have been mentioned as part of the Achaemenid Empire in the following inscriptions:

1. Inscription on Egyptian Statue of King Darius I in the National Museum of Iran.

2. Apadana Palace foundation tablet inscription.
3. Naqsh – e – Rustom Inscription on tomb of King Darius I.

All three inscriptions have been written in Old Persian Cuneiform script.

Hidus have been translated as Hindus since the nasal 'n' before consonant was omitted in the Old Persian Cuneiform script, much like Gandhara is referred to as Gadara. This 'Hidus' province could have been one of the later additions to this empire and if we interpret Maka (one of the provinces mentioned in the Behistun inscription) as corresponding to the Makran coast or the area we today know as Balochistan, then the Hidus province or satrapy could very well be inferred as parts of Sindh region of Pakistan that is located west of River Indus.

According to Herodotus, Indus or Indos as it is called in Greek formed the 20th province or satrapy of the Achaemenid Empire. This Indus could very well be the Hidus province of the above mentioned inscriptions.

> *"The Indians made up the 20th province. These are more in number than any nation known to me, and they paid a greater tribute than any other province, namely three hundred and sixty talents of gold dust."*
>
> **– Histories, Book III, Chapter 94 by Herodotus.**

The following are images of Indian tribute bearer probably carrying gold dust at Apadana Palace, Persepolis (below) and Image of Sattagydian, Gandharan and Hindush warriors (from left to right) in the Naqsh – e – Rostam Inscriptions on tomb of King Xerxes I (below):

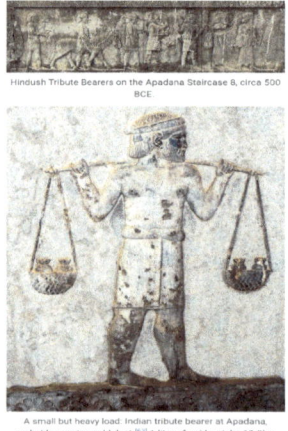

Apadana Palace Foundation Tablets:
The following is the image of the tablet with inscription on it:

Deposition plate of Darius I in Persepolis with the word Hidauv

Also known as DPh inscription, it is written in four identical foundation tablets of gold and silver found in two deposition boxes in foundations of Apadana Palace, Persepolis (capital of Achaemenid Empire). In this inscription, much like the other ones, King Darius I is mentioning extent of his empire. It says:

> *"Darius the great king, king of kings, king of countries, son of Hystaspes, an Achaemenid, King Darius says: This is the kingdom which I hold, from the Sacae who are beyond Sogdia to Kush and from Hidus to Lydia (Sparda). This is what Ahuramazda, the greatest of gods, bestowed upon me. May Ahuramazda protect me and my royal house!"*

– **Naqsh – e – Rustom Inscription on tomb of Darius I:**

The tomb is located near Persepolis and the inscription on it is dated sometime between 490 – 486 B.C. i.e. last years preceding King Darius I death.

> *"King Darius says: By the favour of Ahuramazda, these are the countries which I seized outside Persia; I ruled over them;*

they bore tribute to me; they did what was said to them by me; they held my law firmly; Media, Elam, Parthia, Aria, Bactria, Sogdia, Chorasmia, Drangiana, Archosia, Sattagydia, Gandara (Gadara), India (Hidus), the haoma – drinking Scythians, the Scythians with pointed caps, Babylonia, Assyria, Arabia, Egypt, Armenia, Cappadocia, Lydia, The Greeks (Yauna), the Scythians across the sea (Saka), Thrace, the petasos - wearing Greeks [Yauna], the Libyans, the Nubians, the men of Maka and the Carians."

– **Naqsh – e**
– **Rostam inscription of King Darius I.**

The extent of Achaemenid territories is also affirmed by Strabo (63 B.C. – 24 A.D.), a Greek historian and geographer in his works The Geography (Book XV), Chapter 2, 9 as follows:

"The geographical position of the tribes is as follows: along the Indus are the Paropamisadae, above whom lies the Paropamisus mountain: then, towards the south, the Arachoti: then next, towards the south, the Gedroseni, with the other tribes that occupy the sea – board; and the Indus lies latitudinally, alongside all these places; and of these places, in part, some that lie along the Indus are held by Indians, although they formerly belonged to the Persians."

Thus, we can conclude that the earliest reference to Indian kingdoms pertained to those which were part of Bharatavarsha lying on its peripheries, but became part of the Persian Empire under Achaemenid rule, during reign of one of its King Darius I (522 – 486 B.C.)

II. Earliest literary reference of Indians participating in a War, using War Chariots, War Horses and Iron weapons in recorded ancient history

Herodotus (484 – 425 B.C.) was a Greek historian and geographer who is known for his work 'Histories', a collection of 9 books that give a detailed account of the Greco – Persian wars. He is regarded as one of the earliest historians in recorded ancient history of the world and hence a widely accepted historical figure. The 'Histories' primarily cover the first and second Persian invasion of Greece i.e. events preceding the invasions and the numerous battles that were fought during the invasions. One amongst them was 'Battle of Plataea'.

The Battle of Plataea

It was fought in 479 B.C. towards the end of second Persian invasion of Greece and is the earliest recorded battle in ancient history in which Indians had participated. Sample the following quotes from 'Histories' by Herodotus which gives description of Indians and Gandharans – Daradas (whom Herodotus considered separate and clubbed them with Bactrians instead) who took part in the battle:

"The Indians wore garments of tree – wool and carried bows of reed and iron – tipped arrows of the same. Such was their equipment; they were appointed to march under the command of Pharnazathres, son of Artabates."

– Histories, Book VII, Chapter 65 by Herodotus.

"The Indians were armed in like manner as their foot; they rode swift horses and drove chariots drawn by horses and wild asses."

– Histories, Book VII, Chapter 86 (Excerpts) by Herodotus.

The Bactrians in the army wore a head – gear most like to the Median, carrying their native bows of reed, and short spears. The commander of the Bactrians and Sacae was Hystaspes, son of Darius and Cyrus daughter Atossa."

– Histories, Book VII, Chapter 64 (Excerpts) by Herodotus.

"The Parthians, Chorasmians, Sogdians, Gandarians and Dadicae in the army had the same equipment as the Bactrians. The Parthians and Chorasmians had their commander Artabazus, son of Pharnaces, the Sogdians – Azanes, son of Artaeus, the Gandarians and Dadicae Artyphius, son of Artabanus."

– Histories, Book VII, Chapter 66 (Excerpts) by Herodotus.

"They that were with Xerxes waited for a few days after the sea fight (Battle of Salamis) and then marched a way to Boeotia by the road whereby they had come; for Mardonious was minded to give the king safe conduct, and deemed the time of the year unseasonable for war; it was better he thought to winter in Thessaly, and then attack the Peleponnese in the spring. When they

arrived in Thessaly, Mardonious there chose out first all Persians called Immortals, save only Hydarnes their general, who said he would not quit the king's person; and next, the Persian cuirassiers and the thousand horse, and the Medes and Sacae and Bactrians and Indians, alike their footmen and rest of their horsemen. He choose these nations entire."

**– Histories, Book VIII,
Chapter 113 (Excerpts) by Herodotus.**

"When they were there, they were arranged for battle by Mardonious as I shall show. After the Bactrians, he set the Indians fronting the men of Hermione and Eretria and Styra and Chalcis."

**– Histories, Book IX,
Chapter 31 (Excerpts) by Herodotus.**

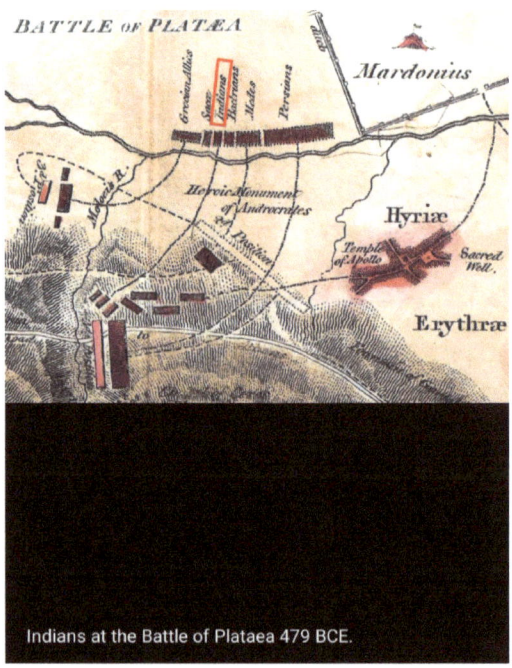

Indians at the Battle of Plataea (above), 479 B.C.

After the defeat of Persians in the naval battle of Salamis (that took place previous year) at hands of the Greeks, the Persian king Xerxes retreated back to Persia with most of his army, but left one of his generals Mardonious under command of 3,00,000 army* to take the battle to the Greek city

– states through land next year. The Persians after failed negotiations, finally encamped at Plataea, Greece. The Greeks numbering around 1,00,000* came out victorious in the decisive battle that followed, routing the Persian army, despite beginning to retreat after taking up positions in surrounding heights overlooking the Persian camp in initial stages of the battle.*[2]

This battle recorded by Herodotus in his works 'Histories' proves beyond doubt that the kingdoms lying on north western peripheries of Bharatavarsha were using:

1. War Chariots.
2. War Horses.
3. Iron Weapons such as Arrows, Spears etc. and strong bows.

well before 5th century B.C. and were adept in it, hence their soldiers were employed by the Achaemenid Empire, thereby forming part of Persian ranks during such military campaigns.

In other words, historicity of the wars and battles which happened in early phase of our recorded ancient history i.e. 'Age of Mahajanapadas' (623 – 323 B.C.), but which were recorded or put down to writing much later (as advent of writing in Bharatavarsha happened in late 3rd century B.C. only), cannot be doubted based upon lack of evidence of Indians using war chariots, war horses, iron weapons etc. and participating in any recorded battles and / or wars of that time which proves their prowess.

There are literary references in our ancient texts of protracted wars that took place in 6th century B.C. in Indian hinterland like the 16 year Magadh – Vajji war that started in 543 B.C., (year of Lord Buddha's death) which will be dealt in detail in coming chapters.

Thus, it can be concluded that the powerful kingdoms of Madhyadesa of Bharatavarsha back in 6th century B.C. like Magadha mahajanapada and Vajji Confederacy led by Licchavi republic clans did have the resources and capability to wage such a prolonged war with each other, which they eventually did and its historicity cannot be doubted upon.

---

[2]Figures as per Herodotus.

CHAPTER 3

THE GANA – SANGHAS OR GANA – RAJYAS OF ANCIENT BHARATAVARSHA

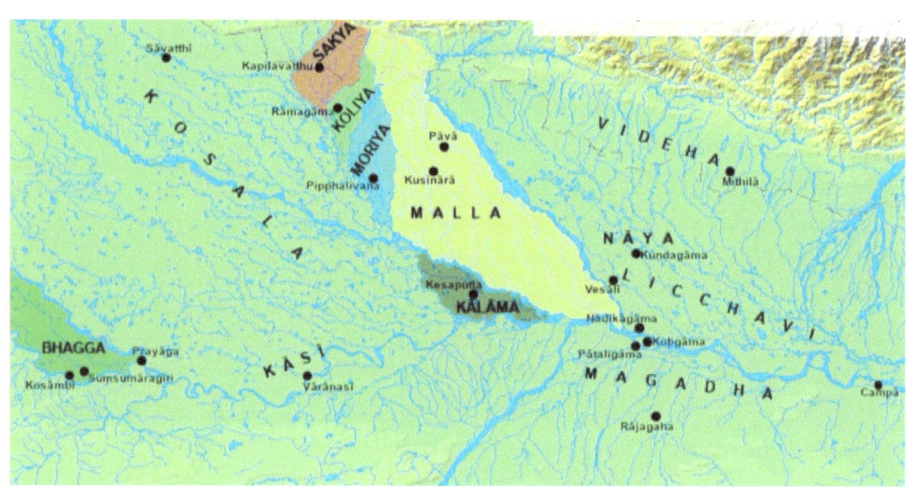

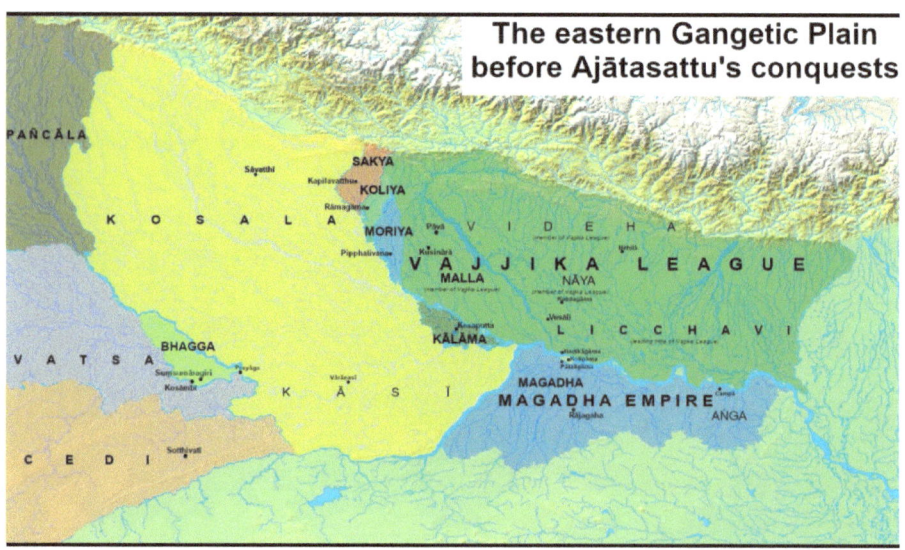

I. The Republics or Gana – Sanghas or Gana – Rajyas of Ancient Bharatavarsha (circa 550 B.C.) were:

1. The Shakyas of Kapilavastu and Lumbini.
2. The Koliyas of Ramagrama.
3. The Moriyas / Mauryas of Pipphalivana.
4. The Videhans of Mithila.
5. The Licchavi clans and Vajji tribe of Vaishali.
6. The Nayaikas or Jnatrikas of Kundagrama and Kollaga
7. The Malla clans of Pava and Kusinara.
8. The Kalamas of Kesaputta
9. The Bhaggas of Sunsamagiri

The ancient Buddhist and Jain texts provide more information on the republics or gana – rajyas than Brahmanacal ones because kingship was central to the Brahmanacal social and political ideology and kinglessness was equated with anarchy. The Brahmanas or Purohitas (priests) may not have enjoyed the same prestige in Gana – Rajyas (whose elites or aristocrats were Kshatriyas alone) as in Rajyas or monarchical kingdoms.

The terms 'Gana' and 'Sangha' were used in literary sources like Panini's Ashtadyayi and the Buddhist text Majjhima Nikaya.

'Gana' refers to a group of men of equal status, 'Sangha' means an assembly and 'Rajya' means governance. Gana – Sangha or Gana – Rajya refers to republican form of governance, but oligarchy in nature i.e. where power rests in hands of few rich and influential families, aristocrats as they are called. Thus, these gana – rajyas cannot be called a democracy because of this reason, though they had certain democratic values in their functioning.

The aristocracy or members of the governing council comprised of heads of leading Kshatriya families. Instead of a hereditary monarch, there was a chief called 'Ganapati, Ganaraja or Sanghamukhya' who met the aristocratic council in a hall called 'Santhagara'. The day to day political management, however must have been entrusted to a smaller group (much like Senate of ancient Roman Republic) within the aristocrats / members.

The fundamental difference between Rajyas or monarchy and Gana – Sanghas were that in the latter, power was diffused, stratification of society on lines of caste, religion, race and ethnicity was comparatively limited and decision making rested on the council instead on the king alone as in case of monarchies. At most in monarchies, the king used to consult his ministers before pronouncing his decision.

A decision was said to have been taken by the council of aristocrats when a proposal proposed by either Sanghamukhya or any other members present was passed when either:

1. Everyone in the council arrived at a consensus to pass it which was called 'Upvahika'.
2. A vote was taken which was called 'chhand' and the majority of the council members voted in favour of the concerned proposal.

Once passed, the proposal could not be tabled back to the council for reconsideration. Lord Mahavira was born in one such aristocratic Kshatriya family in Jnatrika or Nayaika clan.

The Shakyas, one of the most prominent gana – rajyas had their capital at Kapilavastu (modern Piprahwa – Ganwaria). As Lord Buddha belonged to this clan, its details are well documented in buddhist texts which gives significant information on the war, alliances and peace measures. For example, in one of the council meetings, decision on whether to wage a war with neighbouring Koliya gana – rajya over sharing of Rohini river was to be taken. Lord Buddha convinced the council that had assembled at the Santhagara to not wage a war by saying:

"Yes, this is bit of a nuisance, but a war would create a permanent enemy."

King Vidudhaba or Virudhaka of Kosala kingdom soon after coming to power in 543 B.C. by usurping the throne from his father King Prasenjit attacked and annihilated the republican tribes/clans of Shakyas and Koliyas, when he learnt that his mother was a slave girl sent by the Shakyas on purpose. Vidudhaba and his mother Vasabkhatya, daughter of Mahanama (Sanghamukhya of Shakyas) from a slave girl were earlier expelled from Kosala kingdom by the then King Prasenjit for this very reason, but were taken back at Lord Buddha's insistence. Vidudhaba avenged the humiliation first by taking the kingdom from his father, then by annexing both the gana – rajyas into his kingdom.

There were two types of Gana – Rajyas: Those who comprised of one clan like the Shakyas and Koliyas and those who comprised of many clans like the Licchavis and Mallas, who comprised of 9 clans each.

Vajji or Vrijji mahajanapada, one of the 16 mahajanapadas mentioned in ancient Buddhist text Anguttara Nikaya was a confederacy of republican clans.

Vajji Confederacy was thus, a confederacy of many gana – rajyas who had come together to present an united front against a common enemy i.e. Magadha and Kosala mahajanapadas, both of which due to their expansionist policies (Magadha annexed Anga and before that Kosala annexed Kasi) were a constant threat to the small ganarajyas that were touching its borders or were near its borders. Vajji Confederacy consisted of the following republican clans:

1. 9 Licchavi clans (most prominent and most powerful of all gana – rajyas in Vajji confederacy) and the Vajji tribe of Vaishali.
2. 9 Malla clans of Pava and Kusinara.
3. Nayaikas or Jnatrikas of Kundagrama and Kollaga.
4. Videhans of Mithila.

This confederacy was defeated after waging a 16 year war against Magadha mahajanapada (543 B.C. to 527 B.C.) which will be discussed in detail in coming chapters.

Although Kosala kingdom's monarchs King Prasenjit and his son Vidudhaba were matrimonially related to the Magadha kingdom monarchs King Bimbisara[3] and his son Ajatashatru[^], and Magadha – Kosala war did happen before the commencement of Magadh – Vajji war, but contrary to what is mentioned in the Jain Agamas, Kosala kingdom neither was part of the Vajji confederacy nor took part in the Magadh – Vajji war.

The Mallas unlike Nayaikas and Videhans, maintained their sovereignty within the Vajji Confederacy and that is why Anguttara Nikaya mentions them as a mahajanapada, separate from the Vajji Confederacy.

Kautilya's Arthashastra, a treatise on statecraft, outlines the special strategies that a would be conqueror could use to vanquish the gana – rajyas and these were directed towards creating dissension among their ranks.

The strength of the gana – rajyas with respect to their governance structure being best suited for administration of their kingdom became their biggest weakness as the 'everyone has a say in decision making' concept ensured that there was:

1. Delay in taking decisions and / or timely bold decisions and
2. Difference of opinion amongst clans or members of council, failure to arrive at decisions acceptable to all etc,

---

[3] *King Prasenjit's sister Kosala Devi was married to King Bimbisara. ^King Vidudhaba's sister Vajira was married to King Ajatashatru.*

Thereby creating disunity amongst the council or sabha members especially if covertly orchestrated by an enemy kingdom or during sudden invasion by other kingdoms.

The remaining Republics or Gana – Rajyas also got vanquished soon. For example, the Bhaggas of Sunsamagiri became part of Vatsa mahajanapada during King Udayana's rule. The Kalamas of Kesaputta got assimilated into Kosala mahajanapada by its King Vidudhaba. King Ajatashatru also annexed the Moriya gana – rajya of Pipphalivana who might not have been able to give much of a fight after the battle hardened Magadha mahajanapada emerged victorious in the 16 year long Magadh – Vajji war that culminated in 527 B.C.

II. The Licchavis of Vaishali

During the Mahabharata period and later vedic age (900 to 700 B.C.), Videha kingdom of Mithila was a monarchy and its kings used to take the title 'Janaka'. There is no mention of Licchavi clans in the Vedic and Brahmanacal texts pertaining to that period, some of which were orally composed and codified in the realm of Videha by learned scholars such as Uddalaka Aruni, Yajnavalkya, Gargi Vachaknavi etc.

The first mention of Licchavi comes from ancient Buddhist texts which states them to have conquered Videha kingdom and replaced its monarchy with Gana – Rajya or republic, probably somewhere around beginning of 7th century B.C. presumably after weakening or collapse of earlier dispensation as no bloodshed has been mentioned to have taken place in the conquest in any of the ancient texts.

Later they expanded their territory southwards, asserting their suzerainty over other gana – rajyas like Jnatrika / Nayaitrika, Vajji etc and shifted their capital to Vaishali, got organized as a Gana – Rajya and then set up the Vajji Confederacy.

Lord Buddha visited Vaishali multiple times during his lifetime, thereby spending a long time there. He first visited Vaishali during 5th year after his enlightenment i.e. 583 B.C.[4] on being invited by the Licchavis to cure the intestinal disease that had afflicted many inhabitants, caused by decaying bodies as there was a drought prevailing over the region at that time. The Ratna Sutta was recited by Lord Buddha to his disciple Ananda and assembled

---

[4] *Lord Buddha attained enlightenment at 35 years of age i.e. 588 B.C.*

people and all fatal diseases and ailments of the citizens disappeared. These events have been documented in the Buddhist Theravadin commentaries.

On his way to Kusinara in 543 B.C., Lord Buddha delivered his last sermon at Vaishali and announced his Nirvana there. After 100 years of his death, Vaishali held the second Buddhist council in 443 B.C.

The Vajji Confederacy was administered by the Vajji council, which consisted of 18 members of which 9 were from Licchavi clans and rest 9 from Videha, Nayaika / Jnatrika, Vajji and Malla clans together.

Since the 9 Licchavi clans were leading clans of this confederacy, their capital city of Vaishali was the headquarters of the Vajji Confederacy and bulk of the confederate army was made up of Licchavi clan soldiers.

The Licchavis of Vaishali had, according to Ekapana Jataka, 7,707 rajas to govern the realm and a similar number of uparajas (subordinate kings), senapatis (military commanders) and bhandagarikas (treasurers). These figures should not be taken literally but they definitely suggest that the Licchavis had a large assembly comprising the heads of Kshatriya families who called themselves 'Rajas'. They usually met once a year to transact public business and elect their leader who had a fixed tenure. The Licchavi assembly had sovereign power and could pronounce death or exile punishments. Daily administrative matters were dealt by a smaller council of 9 men. Thus, this corporate aspect of governance was held to be major strength of the Licchavi gana – rajya. Shri Rudrapatna Samasastri who was the first person to publish Kautilya's Arthashastra (after he came across manuscripts of antiquity) which he did in Sanskrit to English text in year 1909, referred to or translated gana – rajyas as 'Corporations'.

III. Ganamukhya Chetaka of the Licchavis

At time of Lord Mahavira's birth in 599 B.C., Chetaka was the ganamukhya of the Licchavi ganarajya. He was son of Keka and Yasomati, belonged to the Haiheya clan (which ruled Avanti before Pradyota dynasty) and was one of the 9 elected 'Rajas' of the Licchavi council, highest decision making body. Since, the Licchavis were leading the Vajji Confederacy, and he being leader of the Licchavis also became leader of the confederacy.

He is known for contracting several diplomatic marriages between members of his family and leaders of other republics and kingdoms. Chetaka became a follower of his nephew Lord Mahavira and adopted Jainism.

Marital alliances concluded by Chetaka are as follows:

1. Trishala, his sister married to Vajji council member from Nayaika / Jnatrika ganarajya, Siddhartha who later went on to become father of Lord Mahavira.
2. Prabhavati, his daughter was married to King Udayana of Sindh – Sauvira kingdom.
3. Mrigavati, his daughter was married to King Satanika Parantapa of Vatsa mahajanapada.
4. Siva, his daughter was married to King Pradyota of Avanti.
5. Jyestha, his daughter was married to Nandivardhana of Nayaika / Jnatrika gana – rajya who was also the elder brother of Lord Mahavira.
6. Chellana, his daughter was married to King Bimbisara of Magadha.
7. Padmavati, his daughter was married to King Dadivahana of Anga, who must have been a predecessor of King Brahmadatta, the last ruler of Anga mahajanapada.

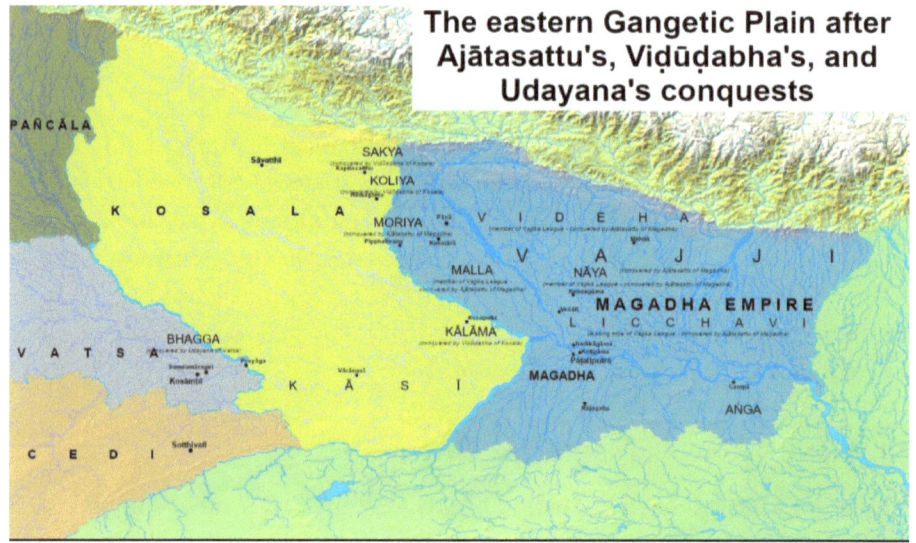

CHAPTER 4

COINS OF ANCIENT BHARATAVARSHA

"The customs of the Lydians are like those of the Greeks, save that they make prostitutes of their female children. They were the first men (known to us) who coined and used gold and silver currency; and they were the first to sell by retail."

– Histories, Book I, Chapter 94 (Excerpts)

Lydia was an ancient kingdom in Asia minor which under its king Alyattes (610 – 560 B.C.) and Croseus (560 – 546 B.C.) controlled all Asia Minor west of river Halys except Lycia down south.

As per Herodotus, ancient Lydians were the first ones to sell produce and products through permanent retail shops which they would have started after minting coins and using them as currency for trade instead of barter system. The Lydian Lion coins which are considered to be the earliest coins to be used as currency were made of electrum (a natural occurring alloy of gold and silver) which were found in Lydia in abundance. It is beleieved they were minted and issued during the reign of King Alyattes i.e. in late 7th century B.C. or early 6th century B.C. But later during the reign of Croseus, sometime around 560 – 550 B.C., gold coins replaced the electrum ones as the standard currency. The Achaemenid gold coins and the Greek gold coins both succeeded the Lydian coins after the kingdom of Lydia got annexed by Persia, under King Cyrus (559 – 530 B.C.). However, the Indian punch – marked silver coins or Karshapanas, as they were called developed independently in early 6th century B.C. and hence were one of the world's first coins to be minted and issued for the purpose of being used as currency, not gift or jewellery.

610–560 BC Lydian electrum coin denominated as ⅓

Excerpts from "Ancient Indian Coinage" by Rekha Jain, 1995, reprinted 2017:

There are a number of numismatists even among the Europeans who did not subscribe to the theory of foreign or late origin of the ancient Indian coinage. EJ Rapson thought that the punch marked coins developed independently of any foreign influence.

"Designs, treatments and die devices (of ancient Indian coins) evince independent thoughts. The Indian figures follow the ideal models of their own land and bear no trace of the conventionalities of Greek art." This was the view of Edward Thomas.

Mr. A. Cunningham did not believe in any foreign influence or origin. Among the Indian numismatists, S.K. Chakraborty is inclined to agree with the view of A. Cunningham that coinage in India evolved in about 800 B.C.

Outside influence started with Persian conquest of Gandhara, Sattagydia, Hidus etc during King Darius I reign (522 – 486 B.C.) as has been discussed in detail in previous chapters. Based upon radiocarbon and other tests, archaeological evidence does not validate this post 522 B.C. date for the Karshapanas presuming trade relations were established with the Persians after their Indus valley conquests and through that influence, coinage in India evolved.

The Later Vedic Literature

The Shatapata and Aitreya Brahamanas and Upanishads which are placed around 900 – 700 B.C. refer to golden metallic pieces such as Niska, Satamana, Pada and Krsnala. They have been mentioned only in connection with the gifts. These seem to be ingots of calculated weight. The transition from this stage to coin proper i.e. as currency happened at advent of the Mahajanapada era (623 B.C.) where coins of recognized weight, measurement etc were issued guaranteed by stamp of authority.

Literary Evidence

The Ashtadhyayi of Panini gives names of number of coins namely Satamana, sana, karshapana, ardhapana or bhaga, pada, dvimasapada, vimsatika and trimsatika. The Buddhist canons and the Jatakas refers to coins kahapana, ardha – kahapana, pada, masaka, adhha masaka and kakini. The Ashtadhyayi dates back to late 4th century B.C. and the Jatakas speak of period 623 to 323 B.C. The Karshapanas are also referred to in some of the 'Dharmasutras' and Jain Agamas which also speaks of events happening during the Mahajanapada era. Thus, from the literary texts, it is clear that the currency became well established by latter half of 6th century B.C. in form of standard weight.

Archeological Evidences

The Bhir Mound hoard of punch marked coins at Taxila, found in the second stratum contained two coins of Alexander, one of Philip Ariaudus which were in mint conditions, besides 1055 silver puch marked coins. Radiocarbon dating puts the date at around 317 B.C. for this hoard and for Chaman Hazuri hoard of greek coins, date is around 400 B.C. The punch marked silver coins found along with the greek and achaemenid gold coins are not of Karshapana series, which proves that the latter were of earlier period.

Northern Black Polished Ware [7th century to 4th century B.C.]

In archaeological excavations at some sites, punch marked coins were found with the Northern Black Polished Ware pottery and other artefacts. NPBW is considered to be pre-Alexandrian. The sites were Rupar III, Purana Qila in Delhi, Ujjain II, Mathura II and Kaushambi. The Carbon – 14 dating also suggests early 6th century B.C. to 5th century B.C. as the date of punch marked silver coins of Karshapana series especially for the ones found in realm of erstwhile Magadha mahajanapada and Kasi – Kosala kingdom.

Metal of the Original Coinage

Among the precious metals, gold alone was well known in the Vedic period. Gold metallic pieces of definite value have been referred to in early vedic and brahmanical texts but only in connection with hoards of money, munificient gifts, jewellery etc. Further golden coins are conspicuous by their non-discovery till now. Silver is rarely referred to except in later Samhitas. Copper was also available. However, copper coins are not known to be of much early period. Cast copper coins probably originated in about beginning of the fourth or at fifth century B.C. Copper punch marked coins were issued around the beginning of the 3rd century B.C. as per P.L. Gupta (Coins, 1969).

On the other hand, the earliest silver coins found at Kasi and Kosala in the gangetic valley and bent bar Shatamana coins found at Gandhara region are of 6th century B.C. The silver was preferred for the manufacture of coins because it served as a better medium of exchange with other regions. Besides, it carried value when melted. As indigenous silver was not available in much quantity, we can surmise that it was being imported from the west (Achaemenid empire).

Quintus Curtis Rufus (1st century A.D.), Roman historian tells us that among the presents given by Ambhi (king of Gandhara kingdom) to Alexander the Great were two hundred talents of Signati Argenti (coined silver money). The coined referred to are the Karshapanas.

The Karshapanas

These were punch marked coins, made of silver that used to be issued by respective mahajanapadas and ganarajyas like Shakyas and other kingdoms locally in 6th century B.C., but later when standard coins of uniform weight and fabric started to be issued by Magadha kingdom sometime around 527 B.C., the same soon became the standard currency throughout Bharatavarsha.

The various ancient regions where coins have been found are:

1. Shurasena (Braj region in and around Mathura).
2. Uttara Panchala (Ahichchatra as capital, corresponds to Rohilkhand region). Ahichchatra is situated in Bareilly district.
3. Dakshin Panchala (Kampilya as capital, corresponds to Bareilly to Chambal region). Kampilya is situated in Farrukhabad district.
4. Vatsa (Kaushambi as capital, includes other regions of Prayagraj district).
5. Kuntala (Karnataka region).

6. Kasi – Kosala (Saketa, Sravasti, Varansasi etc).
7. Malla (Kosia near Gorakhpur and Fazilnagar).
8. Magadha and Anga (Bihar and parts of Jharkhand).
9. Vanga (West Bengal), Kalinga (Orissa), Andhra (River Goadavari and Krishna basins).
10. Asmaka and Mulaka (Telengana and Aurangabad regions).
11. Saurashtra (Kathiawad region).
12. Gandhara (Peshawar, Charsdda and Taxila).

The coins of each of these regions differ from the other in their execution, fabric, weight, quality of metal and symbols.

The region of Shurasena, Uttara Panchala, Dakshina Panchala, Kuntala, Saurashtra and Asmaka used only one symbol on their coins and their symbol differed in their form and execution.

The coins of these regions excluding Asmaka and Kunatala are pieces cut from metal sheets and stamped subsequently. The coins of Asmaka and Kunatala were produced by pouring out molten metal on a flat board and stamping them when the metal was still soft.

The coins of Vatsa, Kosala, Kasi, Magadha, Kalinga and Andhra are thin in fabric and those of Malla and Mulaka are thick and dumpy.

Please note that weight of coins in this chapter have been mentioned in grains. 1 Grain = 64.79891 milligrams.

1. Asmaka Coins
   They are in three distinct weights: 99 to 108 grains, 45 to 58 grains and 21 to 23 grains.
2. Kunatala Coins
   Two types of coins have been found here, one weighing around 105 grains and other 50 grains.
3. Saurashtra Coins
   Coins found in this region are 15 grains in weight.
4. Shurasena and Panchala Coins
   They are of weight standard 25 grains.
5. Gandhara Coins
   These coins (Shatamana or bent bar ones) found at Taxila and Chaman Hazari weigh between 150 to 180 grains.
6. Vanga Coins
   They are between 50 to 52 grains in weight.
7. Vatsa Coins
   They weigh about 50-54 grains.

8. Kosala Coins
   The small sized ones weigh 42 grains. The large sized ones weigh about 79 to 80 grains.
9. Kasi Coins
   The weight of the coins found in this region is around 75 grains.
10. Andhra Coins and Kalinga Coins
    They weigh about 20 grains.
11. Mulaka Coins
    They weigh 65 grains.
12. Malla Coins

The coins of one series appear like dumpy ingots and weigh 65 grains. The coins of other series are of two denominations. The higher denomination weighs 48-50 grains. The lower denomination weighs only 10-12 grains.

Magadha Coins

The coins of Magadha may well be distinguished as belonging to two periods:

1. Those that were issued when Magadha was merely a kingdom i.e. before conquest of Vajji Confederacy was completed in 527 B.C.
2. Those that were issued during its period of imperial expansion and found all over the country or atleast most parts of Bharatavarsha.

The local Magadha coins or pre – expansion period coins are known in three distinct series. They are as follows:

1. Series I: The coins of first series are of two denominations. The higher denomination weighs 125 grains and lower about 3 grains only.
2. Series II: The coins of second series are found in four denominations. The weights are:
   a. 1st denomination: 92-97 grains.
   b. 2nd denomination: 46-49 grains.
   c. 3rd denomination: 13-16 grains.
   d. 4th denomination: 7-8 grains only.
3. Series III: The Magadhan coins of series III are thin, broad pieces similar to coins of Vatsa, Kosala and Kasi. They weigh around 72 grains and bear four well executed bold symbols:
   a. The Sun,
   b. A six armed symbol,
   c. A standing bull and

d. A Lion standing.

These 3 series of coins were issued by the rulers of Magadha when their capital was Girivraja or Rajagriha i.e. during King Bimbisara's reign and early and middle phases of King Ajatashatru's reign.

Standard Magadha Coins

The Magadha monarchs at some stage in late 6th century B.C. finally put a stop to various experimentations with standards of weight and evolved a single denomination full Karshapana silver coin of 32 rattis i.e. 56 grains. These coins were found in the Golakhpur hoard, Patna. These coins consists of five symbols of which the Sun and Six armed symbol are permanent i.e. found in every coin of this type. The coins of Period I from Golakhpur hoard contained 82 percent silver, 15 percent copper and 3 percent of other impurities. The hoard also contained the four symbol Karshapanas which was being used earlier.

Conclusion

Chetaka, ganamukhya of the Licchavis was matrimonially related to both King Pradyota of Avanti mahajanapada and King Satanika Parantapa of Vatsa mahajanapada. King Ajatashatru must have realized this threat. After or just before commencing of the Magadh – Vajji war, as written in ancient Buddhist text Majjhima Nikaya, in order to dissuade King Pradyota from attacking, he built a fortified city near Ganges River which came to be known as Pataliputra. Although he fortified Rajagriha too, but in order to further strengthen hold over his kingdom, he shifted his capital further north to Pataliputra, probably after conclusion of the war but certainly before death of King Pradyota in 527 B.C.

As per the chronology of the punch marked coins provided in the 'Silver Punch marked coins of the Magadha Maurya Karsapana, Series, Bombay, 1985' by P.L Gupta, the new permanent standard of 56 grains, five symbol Karshapana coins, were issued after conclusion of the Magadh Vajji war i.e. in 527 B.C. during King Ajatashatru's reign, which went on to become the standard coin of Magadha kingdom and in due course, most of Bharatavarsha.

Image of Magadha Karshapana coin

CHAPTER 5

THE MAGADH – VAJJI WAR – A MYTHOLOGICAL NARRATION OF A HISTORICAL EVENT

There are three types of conquests that has been mentioned in Arthashastra. They are:

1. Dharmavijaya (Just Conquest)
2. Lobhavijaya (Greedy Conquest)
3. Asuravijaya (Demon like Conquest)

Dharmavijaya

Dharmavijaya, or concept of 'Just conquest' is a conquest which is performed for the sake of protecting dharma or righteousness and destroying those who kill or harm the king's subjects. The Mahabharata war was a Dharma – yudh or a just war in which righteousness prevailed over evil i.e. Dharmavijaya. This type of conquest has been justified and mentioned as one of King's utmost duty or dharma in our sacred texts and other references.

> *"When a king performs a righteous act of violence, they are like great sages. When they slaughter bad people for the sake of dharma, they are not tainted by sin. The king, committed to securing dharma – fostering power by fostering dharma – should punish whoever harms the people. Any action is considered dharma that is commended by noble men who know Vedic lore; anything that they condemn is said to be non – dharma. Understanding dharma and non – dharma, and abiding by the judgement of good men, the king should protect the people well and kill their assailants."*
>
> **– Nitisara, Chapter 6 by Acharya Kamandaki.**

"Ahimsa parmo dharma; Dharma hinsa tathaiva cha."

– Bhagavad Gita

Translation:

Non-violence is the utmost duty, but protecting Dharma (righteousness) is supreme.

Lobhavijaya

Conquests or military campaigns carried out against kingdoms with an intention of extracting some benefits out of the victory from the defeated kingdom such as tribute, taxes, acceptance of suzerainty or overlordship, princess of that kingdom for forced marriage with king or prince of the victorious kingdom etc. comes under Lobhavijaya.

Other Examples:

1. Conquests part of Ashvamedha yagya.
2. Conquests part of Rajasuiya yagya.
3. Conquests part of Digvijaya i.e. conquest of all four quarters which used to be carried out by Chakravartin or emperor of Bharatavarsha.
4. Conquests to prove supremacy over other kingdoms or kings.

Asuravijaya

This type of conquest used to result in annexation of the defeated kingdom by the victorious one. Since the prevalent type of conquest from Mahabharata period till sometime before beginning of the Mahajanapada era was either Dharmavijaya or Lobhavijaya, the concept of Asuravijaya being unheard of, there is no mention of any battle or war in our sacred texts (vedic and brahmanical) that took place during this period which resulted in an Asuravijaya.

The criteria to qualify for performing Rajasuiya yagya was set out as suzerainty over (and subsequent tribute collection from) atleast 100 kings of Bharatavarsha during Mahabharata period because back then, no kingdom of Bharatavarsha used to follow annexation form of conquest because of which there will be no empire which meant that at any given point of time, the hundreds of kingdoms that existed in Bharatavarsha would be intact.

The victorious king in those times did not even disturb the administration of the defeated king's kingdom unless the latter had been killed in the battle or unwilling to continue on the throne in which case his son or any other blood relative will be anointed as king who will then rule as subordinate ally or vassal or satrap of the victorious king.

Example: After killing Jarasandha of Magadha, the Pandavas anointed his son Sahadeva as the king who then fought the Mahabharata war alongside Pandavas, as their ally.

This practice continued even till medieval times especially in Deccan. As per Arab traveler and chronicler Suleiman who visited the court of Mihira Bhoja of Gurjara Pratihara dynasty in 9th century A.D.:

"When a king subdues a neighboring state, he places over it a man belonging to the family of the fallen prince, who carries on the government in name of the conqueror. The inhabitants will not suffer either."

If annexation becomes inevitable, the established religion, laws and customs were to be respected and the new subjects were to be treated as kindly as the old ones.

Kosala mahajanapada annexed Kasi mahajanapada sometime before 623 B.C.

Magadha mahajanapada annexed Anga mahajanapada in early 6th century B.C.

These were the earliest examples of Asuravijaya. Although expansionist policies of both Magadha and Kosala mahajanapadas became evident, still the beginning of imperial expansion age is associated with annexation of the nine gana – rajyas by neighboring monarchial kingdoms Kosala, Magadha and Vatsa in late 6th century B.C.

The Buddhist Tradition [As per Mahaparinibbana Sutta]

There was a diamond mine near a village on the banks of river Ganges, which formed the boundary between both kingdoms of Magadh and Vajji Confederacy. There was an agreement between King Ajatashatru and the Licchavis that they would have an equal share of the diamonds, but because of sheer lethargy, Ajatashatru failed to collect his own share and whole lot of diamonds mined were carried away by the Licchavis.

This happened many times and at last King Ajatashatru got annoyed and thought "It is almost impossible to fight against the whole confederacy of Vajji. I must uproot these powerful Vajjis and exterminate them." He sent his chief minister Vassakara to Lord Buddha to ask him the purpose of Vaishali being invincible to which Lord Buddha, who was in his 80th year i.e. last year (543 B.C.) replied that:

It was not possible to vanquish the Vajjis so long they struck to the following eight principles:

1. They continued to hold public assemblies frequently and timely.
2. They continued to discuss their affairs freely and tried to arrive at unanimity in their resolutions and execution of their affairs.
3. They continued to honour their womanhood, not marrying their daughters forcefully.
4. They continued to honour their elders and advice given by their elders. They continued to respect and worship their elders.
5. They continued their disciplined behavior w.r.t. being punctual at the Santhagara or public assemblies.
6. They continued to act in accordance with the time tested Shastras and enact nothing which is not yet established or goes against already laid down principles.
7. They continued to give protection to Arhats (saints of highest ranks), extend warm welcome and hospitality to them and wish for them to visit again.
8. They continued to worship their Chaityas (Altars) inside Vaishali and do not loot or siphon of the wealth accumulated through these shrines or altars.

Obviously this was the prescription for unity meaning unity is the strength of the Vajji Confederacy. King Ajatashatru seems to have taken a clue from this and prepared for a covert tactic by a carefully planned espionage. He sent his minister Vassakara to Vaishali as a spy to sow dissension or seeds of disunity among the Vajjis in which he succeeded and consequently the Vajji Confederacy was defeated as they could no longer put up a united front against Magadha.

The Arthashastra Verses

1. "The acquisition of the help of corporation is better than the acquisition of an army, a friend, or profits. By means of conciliation and gifts, the conqueror should secure and enjoy the services of such corporation as they are invincible to the enemy and are favourably disposed towards himself. But those who are opposed to him, he should put down by sowing the seeds of dissension among them and by secretly punishing them."

   – Kautilya's Arthashastra, Book XI, Chapter 1, Verse 1.
2. "The corporation of warriors (kshatriyasreni) of Kamboja and Surastra and other countries live by agriculture, trade and wielding weapons. The

corporations of Licchivika, Vrjika, Mallaka, Madraka, Kukura, Kuru, Panchala and others live by the title of a Raja."

— **Kautilya's Arthashastra, Book XI, Chapter 1, Verse 2.**

3. "Spies, gaining access to all these corporations and finding out jealousy, hatred and other causes of quarrel among them should sow the seeds of a well-planned dissension among them and tell one of them: "This man decries you". Spies, under the guise of teachers (Acharya) should cause childish embroils among those of mutual enmity on occasions of disputations about certain points of science, arts, gambling or sports. Fiery spies may occasionally quarrel among the leaders of corporations by praising inferior leaders in taverns and theatres; or pretending to be friends."

— **Kautilya's Arthashastra, Book XI, Chapter 1, Verse 3.**

The above are Verses 1, 2 and 3 of Chapter 1, Book XI of Kautilya's Arthashastra.

The ancient gana – rajyas of Licchavis, Vajjis, Mallas, Kuru etc. no longer existed at time of King Chandragupta Maurya's rule when Arthashastra was written by Kautilya or Acharya Chanakya (also known as Vishnugupta) but still their names have been mentioned in the book's verses in present tense. Corporations meaning gana – rajya have been mentioned as invincible.[5] The strategy of sowing dissension among clans and council members of these gana – rajyas and other gana – rajyas or their confederation to bring their downfall during a war as mentioned in the above verses seems to have been formulated and written based upon such events that actually happened in past.

In other words, the covert strategies adopted by King Ajatashatru during the Magadh – Vajji war finds an indirect mention in the above verses of Arthashastra.

Now, that the historicity of this war has been established beyond doubt, let us study its mythological narration.

The Jain Tradition [As per the Jain Agamas]

Once Queen Padmavati, wife of King Ajatashatru, was sitting in her balcony in the evening. She saw Halla and Vihalla kumaras with their wives sitting on 'Sechanaka' elephant and one of the wives wearing the 18 fold divine necklace. Then she heard one of the maid servants speaking from the garden

---

[5] *The Jain Agamas and Mahaparinibbana Sutta mentions Vajji Confederacy as invincible.*

below "It is Halla and Vihalla kumaras and not the king who enjoy real pleasures of the kingdom", and she thought "what is the use of the kingdom if I do not have both the jewels in my possession?"

So, she shared this thought with King Ajatashatru the same night and became excessively insistent in her demand. King Ajatashatru at last agreed and sent a request to both his brothers to give the elephant and the necklace to him, which both his brothers denied saying that these gifts were given by their dear father, so why should they part from them? King Ajatashatru sent the request thrice but got the same reply all three times. This annoyed him a lot, so he sent his men to arrest them. Meanwhile, Halla and Vihalla kumaras availed a chance and escaped to their maternal grandfather Chetaka, who was king (read as ganamukhya) of the great kingdom of the Vaishali republic (Vajjis). King Ajatashatru sent notice thrice to Chetaka to surrender them but was denied by Chetaka.

This was enough for King Ajatashatru. He called his half brothers Kalakumaras (10 kalakumaras, those born to King Bimbisara and 10 Kali Queens Kali, Sukali, Mahakali etc.) to merge their army with his, since it was well known to King Ajatashatru that Vaishali republic had always been invincible in the past and he alone would not be able to defeat it. Each Kalakumara brought 3000 horses, 3000 elephants, 3000 chariots and 30,000 infantrymen each. On the other hand, Chetaka invited his own allies 9 Mallas, 9 Licchavis and 18 kings of Kasi – Kosala to fight his grandson King Ajatashatru. All those kings came with 3000 horses, 3000 elephants, 3000 chariots and 30,000 infantrymen each, thus all together there were 57,000 elephants, 57000 chariots, 57,000 horses and 5,70,000 infantrymen.

The war began. King Chetaka was a devout follower of Lord Mahavira and had a vow to not shoot more than one arrow per day in a war. It was known to all that Chetaka's aim was perfect and his arrows were infallible. His first arrow killed one Kalakumara, commander of King Ajatashatru. On the consecutive nine days, the rest of the nine Kalakumaras were killed by Chetaka. Deeply sorrowed by the death of their sons, the Kali queens were initiated as nuns in the holy order of Lord Mahavira.

As King Ajatashatru was moving towards defeat, he practiced penance for three days and offered prayers to Sarkrendra and Charmendra (Indra of different heavens), who then helped him in the war. They protected him from the infallible arrow of Chetaka. The war became very severe and by the divine influence of the Indras, even the pebbles, straws, leaves hurled by King Ajatashatru's men were said to have fell like rocks on the army of Chetaka.

This weapon was thus named 'Mahasilakantaka' i.e. the weapon through which more than a lakh people died. Next, the Indras granted a huge, automatically moving chariot with swinging spiked maces and probably blades too on each side, and said to have been driven by Charmendra himself. The chariot moved about in the battlefield crushing lakhs of soldiers. This war chariot was named Rathamusala.

In this battle, Chetaka was defeated but Chetaka and others immediately took shelter inside the city walls of Vaishali and closed the main gate. The walls around Vaishali were so strong that King Ajatashatru was unable to break through them. Many days passed, King Ajatashatru became furious and again prayed to Indra, but this time Indra refused to help him, but King Ajatashatru was informed by an oracle of a demi – goddess "Vaishali can be conquered if Sramana (monk) Kulvalaka gets married to a prostitute."

King Ajatashatru inquired about the monk Kulvalaka and sent for prostitute Magadhika disguised as a devout follower. The fallen woman attracted the monk towards herself and finally the monk gave up his monkhood and married her. Later Magadhika on King Ajatashatru's orders brainwashed Kulvalaka to enter Vaishali disguised as an astrologer. With great difficulty, he did enter Vaishali and learnt that the city was saved by a Chaitya (altar) dedicated to Munisuvrata. Kulvalaka then started telling people that this altar is the reason why this city is suffering through a bad period.

The people uprooted the altar from its very foundation. Kulvalaka gave a signal and King Ajatashatru proceeded as per arrangement. This was the last attack. Vaishali was conquered by King Ajatashatru.

Sechanaka, the elephant died, after it fell in a pit with iron rods and fire made by King Ajatashatru's soldiers. Later, Halla and Vihalla kumaras got initiated as monks in the holy order of Lord Mahavira. King Ajatashatru not only conquered Vaishali, but also Kasi – Kosala.

The Concept of Akshauhini in the Mahabharata Epic

Below mentioned are excerpts from Adi Parva, the first of 18 parvas:

1. Chapter 2, Shloka 13,
   Ugrasravas Sauti brings the concept of Akshauhini before the audience:
   अक्षौहिण्य इति परोक्तं यत तवया सूतनन्दन
   एतद इच्छामहे शरोतुं सर्वम एव यथातथम

Akshauhini is the next thing you have said, O son of Sutananda, and we wish to tell you exactly as it is.

2. Chapter 2, Shloka 14,
   The audience of Rishis ask Ugrasravas Sauti to tell the size of one Akshauhini:

   अक्षौहिण्याः परीमाणं रथाश्वनरदन्तिनाम्
   यथावच चैव नो बरूहि सर्व हि विदितं तव

   Tell us the size of the Akshauhini and the number of the chariots, horses and as well as whatever you know everything.

3. Chapter 2, Shloka 19,
   The number of chariots in one Akshauhini:

   अक्षौहिण्याः परसंख्यानं रथानां दविजसत्तमाः
   संख्या गणित तत्वज्ञैः सहस्राण्य एकविंशति:

   The number of chariots of the Akshauhini was twenty one thousand eight hundred seventy by best of the brahmins who knew the mathematical truth.

4. Chapter 2, Shloka 20,
   Number of elephants in one Akshauhini:

   शतान्य उपरि चैवाष्टौ तथा भूयश च सप्ततिः
   गजानां तु परीमाणम एतद एवात्र निर्दिशेत

   There are twenty one thousand eight hundred seventy elephants (in one Akshauhini).

5. Chapter 2, Shloka 21,
   Number of Infantry in one Akshauhini:

   जज्ञेयं शतसहस्रं तु सहस्राणि तथा नव
   नराणाम अपि पञ्चाशच छतानि तरीणि चानघाः

   I should know a hundred and nine thousand three hundred and fifty men are under one roof.

6. Chapter 2, Shloka 22,
   Number of horses or cavalry in one Akshauhini:

   पञ्च षष्टिसहस्राणि तथाश्वानां शतानि च
   दशोत्तराणि षट पराहुर यथावद इह संख्यया

   Sixty Five Thousand Six Hundred Ten, six Parahur as in number here.

7. Chapter 2, Shloka 23,
   One Akshauhini is known by the number of men as told below:

   एताम अक्षौहिणीं पराहुः संख्या तत्त्वविदो जनाः
   यां वः कथितवान अस्मि विस्तरेण दविजोत्तमाः

which I have told you in detail, O best of the Brahmins.
8. Chapter 2, Shloka 24,
   Total number of Akshauhinis that participated in the Mahabharata war were 18 (11 from Kauravas side and seven from Pandavas side):
   एतया संख्यया ह्य आसन् कुरुपाण्डवसेनयोः
   अक्षौहिण्यो द्विजश्रेष्ठाः पिण्डेनाष्टादशैव ताः
   With this numbers, the Akshauhinis of the Kaurava and Pandava armies, the best of Brahmins are eighteen in body.

As per the Jain Agamas,

The number of soldiers fielded in the Magadh Vajji war were:

I. From Chetaka or Vajji Confederacy side,
= 5,70,000 (Infantry) + 57,000 (Elephants) + 57,000 (Horses) + 57,000 (Chariots)
= 7,41,000.
It is written that King Ajatashatru merged his army with the ones brought by the 10 Kalakumaras, but exact strength of his army has not been mentioned. For calculation sake, let us presume it was equal to the one fielded by the 10 Kalakumaras together. This implies that:

II. From King Ajatashatru's side or Magadha Mahajanapada's side,
= {3,00,000 (Infantry) + 30,000 (Elephants) + 30,000 (Horses) + 30,000 (Chariots)}*2
= 7,80,000.
Total number of soldiers who participated in the Magadh – Vajji war at Vaishali:
= 7,41,000 + 7,80,000
= 15,21,000.
Casualties or number of soldiers who died in this war = In Lakhs (exact number not mentioned).

As per the Mahabharata Epic,

The total number of soldiers who participated in the Mahabharata war at Kurukshetra:
= 18 Akshauhinis

= {1,09,350 (Infantry) + 21,870 (Elephants) + 65,610 (Horses) + 21,870 (Chariots)}*18

= 2,18,700 (Strength of one Akshauhini) * 18

= 39,36,000.

As per the epic, only twelve warriors amongst all who participated survived the war which means,

Casualties or number of soldiers who died in this war

= 39,36,000 - 12

= 39,36,588.

Names of twelve survivors are:

1. Lord Krishna.
2. The five Pandavas namely Yudhishtira, Bheema, Arjuna, Nakula and Sahadeva.
3. Yuyutsu (son of Dhritarashtra and maid Sukda).
4. Satyaki, one of Yadava clan warriors.
5. Kritivarman (commander – in – chief of the Narayani Sena).
6. Ashvattama (son of Dronacharya).
7. Kripacharya.
8. Vrishaketu (youngest son of Karna who fought alongside Pandavas).

According to Roman writer Pliny (23 A.D. – 79 A.D.), King Chandragupta Maurya of the Mauryan dynasty who ruled from 323 B.C. to 297 B.C., possessed an army of 6 lakhs infantry, 30,000 cavalry and 9000 elephants. The vast area that he ruled included present day Pakistan, Afghanistan, North, Central, Western and Eastern India. The casualties in the Magadh – Kalinga war that took place in 261 B.C., during King Ashoka's reign is said to have been 1 lakh as per one of the Rock Edicts of King Ashoka of Magadha kingdom. This war was the bloodiest of its time. King Ashoka is believed to have given up further military conquests seeing the bloodshed in the Magadh – Kalinga war.

Even if we presume that the society during those times in our Indian subcontinent and nearby places was highly martial, still it is impossible for even quarter of the total numbers mentioned in the Jain Agamas and Mahabharata epic to have actually participated in the respective wars.

In Mahabharata war, almost all kingdoms of Bharatavarsha has been mentioned in the epic to have participated which means this war happened comparatively on a large scale, numerically. Still given that the human population of our subcontinent 3000 – 3500 years BP (before present) was very less than what it is now, a fraction probably, the figures mentioned in the epic is highly improbable, an exaggeration of course.

Hence, the number of casualties and strength of armies in Magadh – Vajji war and the Mahabharata war (as mentioned in the Jain Agamas and Mahabharata epic) are highly exaggerated. Such inaccuracies create an impression of the event being a 'myth' and description of the event in a mythological way casts doubt on its historicity, unless of course, its happening can be proven beyond doubt.

Both the weapons 'Mahasilakantaka' and 'Rathamusala' or scythed chariot were weapons developed and introduced to warfare for the first time in history of the world in Bharatavarsha. There is nothing divine about it. The catapult engine or Mahasilakantaka, throwing boulders has been used to break fort walls during siege in recorded history. The Ottomans used such a weapon against Byzantines in 'Siege of Constantinople' in 1453 A.D. and it turned the tide of the battle in favour of the Ottomans.

There were no pebbles, straws or leaves hurled. It has been written in this way to show that the weapon was extremely effective in causing mayhem on the enemy side.

The Battle of Megiddo

This battle fought between Egyptian forces under the command of Pharaoh Thutmose III and a large rebellious coalition of Canaanite vassal states led by King of Kadesh on 16th April 1457 B.C., is the first battle in recorded history of the world which has been documented in a relatively reliable manner, the way Magadh – Vajji war is considered the first war or a series battles to be recorded in detail in ancient history of Bharatavarsha.

All details of Battle of Megiddo come primarily from the hieroglyphic writings on the Halls of Annals in the Temple of Karnak, Thebes (Luxor), by the military scribe Tjaneni. It even gives the casualty figures.

Conclusion:

The question is had the number of soldiers fielded by both sides at the Battle of Megiddo been exaggerated and had there been primacy given to God and religion, mention of too many divine interventions, use of celestial weapons or Divya – Astras and events ascribed to divinity or Gods as in case of Magadh – Vajji war or Mahabharata, then would the information still be reliable enough to prove its historicity?

Answer is No, as modern historians would have given it a tag of mythology to it thereby fictionalizing a historic event.

Since the Jain Agamas were written in 3rd century B.C. after the advent of writing in India during King Ashoka's reign, the description of a historical event had got corrupted or had been manipulated in a way that it gives primacy to the religion and their Gods like personal intervention of Lord Indra in the war and providing divine help.

Take the 'Battle of Ten Kings' of Rig Veda for instance. It also has similar narration where Lord Indra himself helps King Sudas and his Bharata tribe to destroy fortifications of the Dasyu tribes by personally taking part in the battle and using divine weapons for this purpose.

This style of writing is not something new or one – off when it comes to Indian Literature especially ancient sacred texts. The Mahabharata epic records the Mahabharata war and prelude to the war at Kurukshetra in a very intricate manner, recording even the minutest of details, but still it is called a Mythology and the war a 'Mythological war' and not historic.

The Mahabharata epic recited by Ugrasravas Sauti, a bard or professional storyteller is of 1,00,000 verses which got orally codified to its current form at the Naimishara or Naimisaranya forest's twelve year gathering of sages during the reign of either Satanika I (son of Janamejaya) or his son King Aswamedhadatta, within 100 years of happening of the war. The corruption or manipulation in explaining this historical event must have occurred at this oral codification time which was then transmitted to successive generations orally till it was put down to writing for the first time in Sanskrit Brahmi script (and not Prakrit or Tamil Brahmi script) and was written sometime between 185 B.C. to 149 B.C., during the reign of King Pushyamitra Shunga of Magadha kingdom (as explained in Part II, Chapter 1 of this book).

If we remove the divine interventions and events that have been ascribed to divinity from the Mahabharata epic and consider its mention of exaggerated number of soldiers who participated and died in the great war as conforming to the prevalent style of writing rather composing of that time in Bharatavarsha, then **we can conclude that the epic and the war at Kurukshetra were indeed historic. As it is referred to in Puranas, it is our Bharatavarsha's 'Itihasa'.**

Archaeological evidences like excavation of coins (hoards of them at some places) belonging to 6th century B.C. or prior in and around capitals and important cities of:

1. Major kingdoms i.e. Mahajanapadas.
2. Smaller kingdoms i.e. Janapadas (e.g. Vanga, Mulaka and Kuntala).
3. Gana – rajyas or Republics (e.g. Shakyas).

Proves beyond doubt that these kingdoms and republics co-existed together during the time of Lord Buddha (623 – 543 B.C.).

Many of these kingdoms mentioned in ancient Buddhist and Jain texts like Anguttara Nikaya, Digha Nikaya and Vyaka Prajnapati or Bhagvati Sutra also finds mention in the Mahabharata epic. They also have been mentioned in the epic to have participated in the great war.

Example: Kuru, Panchala, Gandhara, Magadha, Chedi, Kekaya, Madra – Kshudraka, Matsya, Shurasena, Sindh – Sauvira etc.

The Mahabharata epic does not mention any cities of importance in Indus Valley civilization like Harappa, Mohenjodaro etc. Instead it mentions the following kingdoms in the same geography:

1. Sindh Sauvira ruled by King Jayadaratha.
2. Gandhara ruled by Shakuni.
3. Madra ruled by Shalya.
4. Kekaya, Salwa and Ambastha.

This proves that the Mahabharata war must have happened well after the collapse or decline of the Indus Valley or Harappan civilization i.e. after 1500 B.C. as a continuity gets established till advent of the Mahajanapada era (623 – 323 B.C.).

PART III

FROM AN ARCHAEOLOGICAL PERSPECTIVE

CHAPTER 1

IRON METALLURGY IN ANCIENT BHARATAVARSHA

*I*ron melts at 1540°c, which is quite high. One way to produce an engineered structure is to melt iron and then cast the molten iron into prefabricated moulds, so that after the metal solidifies, it takes shape of the mould. This material manufacturing process is called Casting. We shall discount the casting technique in the Indian context because the ancient Indian furnaces were not capable of reaching such a high temperature. It is also well established that ancient Indians did not really work with liquid iron.

Operation of the Bloomery Furnace

The ancient Indian furnaces are called bloomery furnaces because the end product was an iron bloom. Preheating facilitated breaking of the iron ores and the fine dust separated by washing or by wind. The preheated iron ore and charcoal were charged in alternating layers, the furnace ignited and slowly heated to the reduction temperature (1000°c to 1200°c). Different designs of iron extraction furnaces have been described in literature. Their heights ranged between 2m and 6m. While some of the liquid slag flowed out of bloomery furnace during the reduction of iron ore to iron, some of it still remained when the hot iron lumps were take out of the furnace. Therefore, the hot lumps that were extracted from the bloomery furnace at end of the heat (typically lasting for about six to eight hours) were immediately hammered. In this process, most of the entrapped liquid fayalitic slag flowed out of the solid reduced iron mass. However, it was not possible to remove all entrapped liquid slag and therefore ancient irons produced by the direct reduction process always contained entrapped inclusions composed mainly of fayalites, iron oxides and glassy phases.

The relatively small iron lumps produced in the bloomery furnace were the starting materials for the manufacture of large iron objects in general. The lumps were also used after suitable heat treatments for manufacturing agricultural tools (spades, sickles and weeding forks), household items (knives, ladles, spoons, sieves, saucepans, cauldrons, bowls, dishes, saucers etc.), building tools (nails, clamps, staples, sheets, door handles and spikes), other artefacts (hammer, anvils, scissors, saws, chains) and warfare weapons (swords, javelins, armour, helmets and shields).

The second urbanization of India (that is settlements along the Ganga) was strongly influenced by the steeling of iron.

Sanskrit literary sources (for instance the Rasa Ratna Samuchchaya dated to $8^{th} – 12^{th}$ century A.D.) classify iron into three basic categories: Wrought iron (kanta loha), carbon steel (tikshna loha) and cast iron (munda loha). The Rasendrashahr Samgraha again mentions these three classifications and also states that 'Munda is ten times better than iron rust, Tikshna is hundred times better than Munda, and Kanta million times better than Tikshna iron'. These three basic categories were further classified according to carbon content, heat treatment and end use.

Munda was of three varieties:

Mridu, which melts easily and does not break and is glossy. Kuntha, which expands with difficulty when struck with hammer. Kadara, which breaks down when struck with hammer and has a black fractured surface.

Six varieties of Tikshna have been provided:

Khara, Sara, Hrinnala, Tarabatta, Bajira and Kalaauha.

Five varieties of Kanta were recognized:

Bhramaka, Chumbaka, Karshaka, Dravaka and Romakanta. The variety of iron which makes all iron move was called Bhramaka, that which kisses iron was called Chumbaka, that which attracts iron was called Karshaka, that which at once melts was called Dravaka, and Romakanta was the kind when broken shoots forth hair like filaments.

The Wootz Steel

"One of the greatest material discoveries to originate from the Indian subcontinent is 'Deccani Wootz Steel' often referred to as "the wonder material of the Orient"."

– **Sachse, 1994 and Srinivasan and Ranganathan, 2004.**

This was the material from which the famed Damascus blades were made. The high quality wootz swords, knives and armour were artistically embellished with carvings and inlays of brass, silver and gold. Wootz steel is primarily iron containing a high percentage of carbon (1.3% - 1.8%). It should be mentioned the term steel used in modern parlance normally mentions an alloy of iron and carbon. By this definition, most of the bloomery iron, after being refined and carburized in the smithy, has enough carbon to be called Steel. The term wootz should therefore be used only for the high carbon alloy produced by the crucible melting process.

Wootz steel is thus a ferro – carbon alloy with partially and heterogeneously spherodised cementite, with carbon contents between 1.3% - 1.8%. In order to process wootz steel cakes into fine swords, the the wootz discs were cut open longitudinally. They were then skillfully worked through several stages by beating, tempering, sharpening and finally etching the surface. This required very careful control of metallurgical parameters.

The ancient Indians mastered the complexities involved in both special steel production and their processing into fine cutting edge objects. The high carbon containing wootz steel cakes were manufactured in the Deccan in large amounts and were shipped to centres of sword production in India and all over the Middle – East during the medieval period.

The surface of the blade showed an intricate wavy pattern, the best jauhar (pattern) being the circles and waves popularly called 'Lahriyadar'. There also exist complete manuals on this craft, called the 'Shamshernamas'. The manufacture of wootz cakes and fabrication of swords from these cakes, were known even prior to the arrival of Muslims in India. This is attested by large number of iron and steel weapons discovered routinely by archaeologists in Andhra Pradesh and Karnataka. The Deccani Kakatiyas were renowned for their swords and swordsmanship.

Quintus Curtis Rufus (1st century A.D.), a Roman historian, mentions that a present of steel cakes was made to Alexander the Great by Porus in 323 B.C., whose country he had invaded.

> *"We can hardly believe that a matter of about thirty pounds weight of steel would have considered a present worthy of acceptance by the conqueror of (known) world, had the manufacture of that substance been practiced by any nations of the West in the days of Alexander."*
>
> – **Neogi (1914)**

> *"There is no evidence to show that any of the nations of antiquity, besides the Hindus were acquainted with the art of making steel. The references to iron by Greek and Latin writers reveal their ignorance not understanding. Although they refer to the qualities of steel, they never refer to the method by which it was prepared from iron."*

– Neogi (1914)

Ashokan pillars, which have been stone cut in a faultless manner from large blocks of stone, must have been possible with the use of the finest steel saws and steel chisels in India in the 4th century B.C. (read 3rd century B.C.). The use of a large number of surgical instruments quoted in Sushruta Samhita (3rd century B.C.), some of which 'could bisect a hair longitudinally', also points to the use of steel in India in making surgical instruments in pre – Christian times.

Carburization was known to Indians quite early in history. Ghosh and Chattopodhyay (1982), have reported an iron sickle found at Barudih in Bihar dated to 810 B.C. It contained 0.35% Carbon, 0.2% Si, 0.2% S, 0.5% P and 0.04% Mn. Hadfield (1912) had analyzed several iron objects from Taxila and found them to contain 1.3% - 1.5% carbon; 1.23% in one of the samples, high carbon percentage being their feature.

> "But of all varieties of iron the palm goes to the Seres with their fabrics and skins. The second prize goes to Parthian iron; and indeed no other kinds of iron are forged from pure metal, as all the rest have a softer alloy welded with them."
>
> – Pliny (1st century A.D.)

> "The Seres are Tamil Cheras of South India. The large number of Roman coins found in Chera territory attests to the robust trade of Deccanis with the Romans. The Tamil Cheras of South India are known to have been wootz steel producers from at least the 3rd century B.C. based on recent archaeological finds."
>
> – Rajan 1989-90, Craddock, 1998; Srinivasan and Griffith, 1997)

Rasaratnasamucharya's bluish black Kalayasa (5.82) which had been mentioned earlier in Kautilya's Arthashastra (2.17.14) corresponded beautifully with the Damascus sword (as the Europeans called it) – 'the sharpened edges which do not get spoiled by hammering'. It thus establishes Bharatavarsha's primacy not only in wootz but also in finished steel.

> "Very few excavations of wootz production sites have been conducted in India. The few studies indicate crucible steel dated 250 B.C. in Tamil Nadu. **The site at Kodumanal is dated to the 3rd century B.C. It is the earliest dated site containing crucibles that were used for wootz steel production.**"

– Rajan 1989-90, Craddock, 1998; Srinivasan and Griffith, 1997)

It is therefore Bharatavarsha, where the story of 'steel' begins.

CHAPTER 2

BEGINNING OF IRON AGE IN BHARATAVARSHA AND ITS MAHABHARATA CONNECTION

The Painted Grey Ware Culture

The Painted Grey Ware Culture is an Iron Age culture of the Gangetic Plain and Ghaggar – Hakra valley or banks of dried up Saraswati river in the Indian subcontinent, conventionally dated 1300 B.C. to 800 B.C. From archaeological perspective, iron artefacts and / or weapons have been found in excavations carried on following Mahabharata sites dating back to PGW period, excavated along with PGW pottery and other artefacts:

1. Bhagwanpura in Kurukshetra (near Saraswati river).
2. Indraprastha (or Delhi especially Purana Qila) or Khandavaprastha.
3. Panipat.
4. Sonipat.
5. Baghpat (including Sinauli, where ancient chariot has been excavated).
6. Hastinapura, near Meerut (capital of Kuru kingdom).
7. Tilpat.
8. Ahichchatra, situated in Bareilly district of Uttar Pradesh, capital of Northern Panchala ruled by King Ashvattama.
9. Kampilya, situated in Farukhabad district of Uttar Pradesh, capital of Southern Panchala ruled by King Dhrupad.
10. Mathura, capital of Shurasena kingdom or Yadavas.
11. Bairat or Viratnagar, capital of Matsya kingdom ruled by King Virat (a town in Kotputli – Behror district of Rajasthan.
12. Kaushambi, capital of Vatsa kingdom (after the Kurus shifted their capital due to gangetic floods in Hastinapura.
13. Banawali, (on banks of Saraswati river) in Fatehabad district, Harayana.

As per oral tradition, the five villages that Lord Krishna asked on behalf of the Pandavas to avert the Mahabharata were:

1. Indraprastha (Delhi).
2. Swarnaprastha (Sonipat).
3. Panprastha (Panipat).
4. Vyaghrprastha (Baghpat).
5. Tilprastha (Tilpat).

Excerpts from Indraprastha (2021) by B.B. Lal (Archaeologist):

As a result of the exploration, we found that it is the Painted Grey Ware culture which is the lowest common denominator at all sites associated with the Mahabharata story as shown in following map:

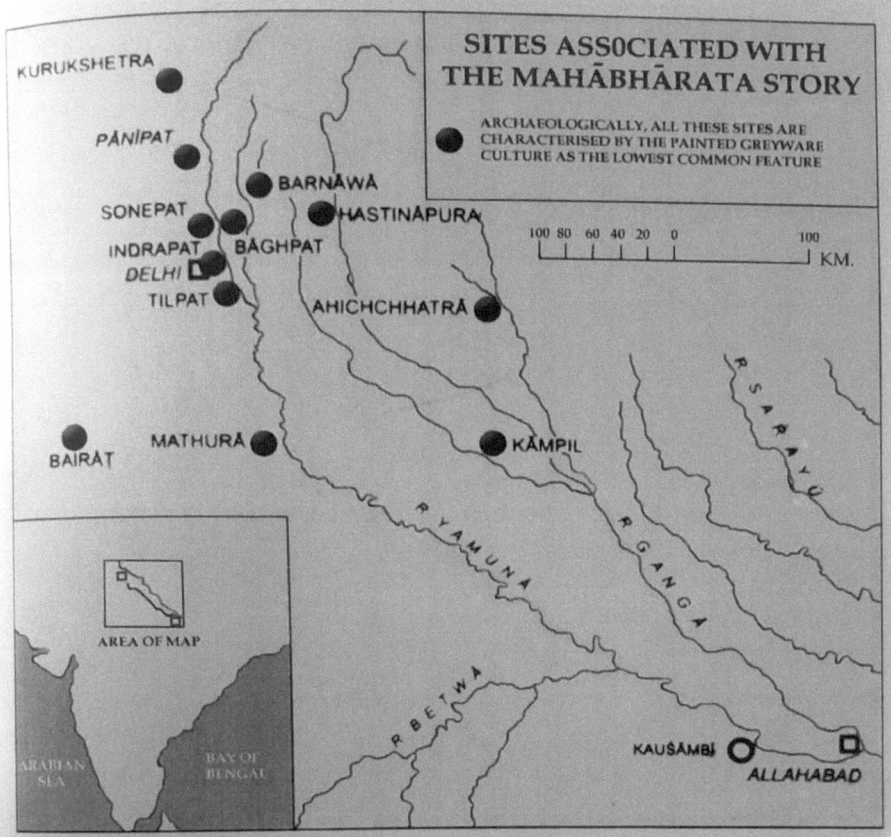

In fact, even sites associated with the story through oral tradition have yielded remains of the Painted Grey Ware culture. For Example, the five villages mentioned above to avert the war.

Amidst metal, besides copper, iron was in full use. The collective evidence from various PGW sites shows the manufacture of domestic objects like axes, nails, hooks, tongs etc. in addition to arrowheads, spearheads, daggers etc. which may have been used in warfare.

Jodhpura in Rajasthan has brought to light a furnace with a side hole through which the nozzle of bellows could have been inserted to pump in air for increasing the heat. It may incidentally be noted that the use of iron by PGW people was in marked contrast to the Harappans who did not know this metal. However, recent findings in Ahichchatra push PGW culture period back by two centuries to 1500 B.C. [As per "On the botanical findings from excavations at Ahichchatra, a multicultural site in Upper Ganga Plain, U.P." (2015) by Anil K Pokharia, Chanchala Srivastava, Bhuvan Vikram].

Recent excavations in Central Ganga Plains of U.P., has turned up iron artefacts, furnaces and weapons dating from 1800 – 1400 B.C. thereby predating the conventionally accepted PGW culture period. These excavated sites are:

1. Raja Nala-ka-Tila, Sonbhadra district, U.P.
2. Malhar, Chandauli district, U.P.
3. Daudpur, Lucknow district, U.P.

Excerpts from "The Origins of Iron Working in India: new evidence from the Central Ganga Plain and the Eastern Vindhyas", by Archaeologist Rakesh Tiwari published in Antiquity, Volume 77, Issue 297, September 2003:

1. Raja Nala-ka-Tila
   Evidence for iron working include iron artefacts such as a nail, chisel, knife and arrowhead. Radiocarbon dates for the iron bearing deposits range between 1400 and 800 B.C.
2. Malhar
   It is a hematite rich terrain situated on banks of Karamnasa river. Identified finds include a nail, clamp, spear-head, arrow-head, awl, knife, bangle, sickle and plough. Also, there was iron slag, tuyeres and several elongated clay structures, with a burnt internal surface. The presence of coarse variety of corded potsherds implies that the iron appeared earlier earlier here than in Raja Nala-ka-Tila's 1400 – 800 B.C. period. **This assumption was endorsed by two radiocarbon dates ranging around 1800 B.C.**
   The area around Malhar may have been something of a centre of iron production. A small mound of a kind locally known as lohsan or lohsanwa, about 500 m south to the main site of Malhar, on excavation revealed two damaged clay furnaces filled with iron slag, an axe and

tuyeres. More clay furnaces in damaged condition were unearthed in several other Lohsanwa sites such as Phakkada Baba and Naugarh Kot. The extraordinary concentration of iron slag heaps at these sites suggest that iron smelting activities continued at these sites for a long time. Nearby Geruwatwa Pahar areas appears to have been a major source of iron ore. It is full of hematite. Villagers reported (as a tradition passed down from several generations) that 'Agarias' (a particular tribe known for iron smelting skills) from Robertsganj side, used to come in this area to procure iron by smelting the hematite. Probably, hematite was being primarily smelted at the Baba wali Pahari or Phakkada Baba and carried over to Karamnasa valley sites (situated at distance of 6-8 km) for secondary smelting. Thus, this part of Karamnasa valley would have been a regional centre for iron production and the Malhar, a workshop – site for the manufacturing of the iron artefacts.

3. Daudpur

   Daudpur is in the valley of Sai, a minor Ganga tributary near Lucknow. The excavations at this site consists of Iron Artefacts such as arrow-head dating to around 1700 B.C.

Iron artefacts from Raja Nala-ka-Tila (above left) and damaged circular clay furnace at lohsanwa mound, Malhar (above right).

There is no logical basis to connect the beginning of iron in India with any diffusion from the west, from Iron and beyond and further that India was a separate and possibly independent centre of manufacture of early iron. **The date of beginning of Iron smelting in India may well be placed as** early as 16th century B.C. and by about early decade of 13th century B.C. iron smelting was definitely known in India on a bigger scale.

References of Use of Iron in the Mahabharata Epic

1. Book 1: Adi Parva: Khandava-daha Upa Parva: Section CCXXVII:
   "Pavaka then gave unto Krishna, a discuss with an iron pole attached to a hole in the centre. It was a fiery weapon and became his favourite. Having obtained that weapon, Krishna also became equal to the task."
   Pavaka, son of Agni-deva (God of Fire) had given Lord Krishna, a new celestial weapon which came to be known as Sudarshana Chakra, which was made of iron, at least part of it.
2. Book 3: Vana Parva: Indralokagamana Upa Parva: Section LI
   "And amongst them will move that great warrior Bhima of terrible prowess, armed with his iron mace held on high and capable of slaying every warrior."
   Maces were mainly made of iron.
3. Book 3: Vana Parva: Teerth Yatra Upa Parva: Section CLXXII
   "And battered and broken by the straight coursing iron shafts, shot by me, the city of the Asuras, O king, fell to the earth. And they also wounded by my iron arrows, having the speed of thunder, began O monarch, to go about, being urged by destiny."
   Arrows were mainly made by iron.
4. Book 4: Virata Parva: Gau Harana Upa Parva: Section LXII
   "And loud was the clatter made by Arjuna's shafts as they cleft the coats of mail belonging to mighty warriors made of steel, silver and copper. And the field was soon covered with corpses of warriors mounted on elephants and horses, all mangled by the shafts of Partha of great impetuosity like unto sighing snakes."
   Coats of Mail refers to an armour composed of metal rings or plates. Sometimes, the arrows were also made of steel, silver and copper.
5. Book 1: Adi Parva: Viduragamana Upa Parva: Section CCIX
   "There were also large iron wheels planted on them. And with all these was that foremost of cities adorned. The streets were all wide and laid out excellently; and there was no fear in them of accident. And decked with innumerable mansions, the city became like unto Amaravati and came to be called Indraprastha (like unto Indra's city)."
   Wheels of Chariots were made of iron.

6. Book1: Adi Parva: Khandava-daha Upa Parva:
   "And there came also desirous of battle, innumerable Asuras with Gandharvas and Yakshas and Nagas sending forth terrific yells. Armed with machines vomiting from their throats iron balls and bullets and catapults for propelling huge stones, and rockets, they approached to strike Krishna and Partha, their energy and strength increased by wrath."

Catapults refer to Mahasilakantaka type catapult engine (See Part II, chapter 5). The iron balls may refer to canon balls made of iron or such weapon highly advanced for its time.

The above English translation and interpretation of shlokas from Mahabharata epic proves iron was being used widely in those times for making weapons and other equipments such as chariot wheels.

This means the Mahabharata war could not have taken place before iron smelting was known in India i.e. could not have taken place before 1800 B.C.

CHAPTER 3

THE HASTINAPURA FLOODS, INDRAPRASTHA AND KAUSHAMBI EXCAVATIONS

Excerpts from Indraprastha by B.B.Lal (Archaeologist), 2021:

The Mahabharata mentions that the Kauravas invited the Pandavas to the game of Chaupar / Chausar at which the latter lost all they had, including their wife Draupadi. This scene is depicted in the paintings of Razmnama, a Persian translation of the Mahabharata, made during the reign of Akbar. The painting shows the chaupar board in the middle and players around it.

The Hastinapura Floods, Indraprastha And Kaushambi Excavations

A painting from Razmanama, showing the Kauravas and Pandavas playing the game of chaupar (above).

The game requires a board which is in form of a cross made of cloth; gamesmen which are made of wood and plano – convex in shape; and dice made of ivory or wood and oblong in shape having 1,2,3, and 4 blind holes on the sides.

The excavations of PGW sites have yielded plano – convex gamesmen in terracotta and oblong dice in bone bearing the required numbers. Both the figures are shown below. Owing to the climatic conditions of the country, survival of a board of cloth is doubtful.

We return to the excavation at Hastinapura. What we found was intriguing. While the PGW deposits were duly encountered in the western part of the mound, these were missing from the eastern part, which faced the Ganga. A question came to my mind: Could the river have cut away the eastern part of the settlement?

And lo! We found the evidence of a mighty flood. A flood in Ganga did destroy a considerable part of the settlement. While most of the eroded material must have been carried away with the flood, some of it got deposited close to the erosion scar. While most of the dislodged material must have been carried away by the furious flood, it is just likely, we thought, that some of it may have stuck up at the bottom of the dried up river bed of past course of Ganges river. With this hypothesis, we dug four bore-holes in the river bed and would you believe found a small portion of the washed away material at a depth of 15 metres below the surface. It includes pottery associated with the PGW culture.

It is interesting to find that the archaeological evidence of a flood having destroyed Hastinapura is duly corroborated by ancient literature. The Matsya and Vayu Purana gives a genealogical list of the Paurava or Bharata

– kula dynasty. It begins with Parikshit, son of Abhimanyu, who ascended the throne after the Mahabharata war. Fifth in the list is Nichakra about whom the text says:

Gangayapahrite tasminnagare Nagasahavaye /
Tyakva Nichaksurnagaram Kausamyams a nivatsyati //

i.e. When the city of Nagashvya (Hastinapura) is carried away by Ganga, Nichakra will abandon it and dwell in Kaushambi.

We have already noted the destruction of Hastinapura by a flood in the Ganga. The point now remains is about the shifting of the capital to Kaushambi. Excavations at this site has shown that the settlement over here began with a kind of Painted Grey Ware which is devolution of the crisp PGW found in the lower levels of Hastinapura. In fact, in the upper levels of Hastinapura itself, this kind of degeneration was noticeable. Thus, the uppermost levels of Hastinapura are easily correlatable with the beginning of Kaushambi.

> However, the Kuru kingdom did not cease to exist after King Nichakra of Bharata – kula dynasty shifted his capital from Hastinapura to Kaushambi, thereby creating a new kingdom in the lower Gangetic doab called Vatsa. The Kuru kingdom that was left behind later became a republic or gana – rajya as per Kautilya's Arthashastra.

As is well known, the Jatakas relate to the previous births of the Buddha. So, it is reasonable to presume that its stories pertains to prior to lifetime of Lord Buddha i.e. before 623 B.C.

The very first sentence of the Sambhava Jataka states "Once upon a time a king called Dhananjaya Korabya reigned in the city of Inderpatta in the Kuru kingdom." There are three assertions to it:

1. There was a Kuru kingdom.
2. There was a city in this kingdom, named Inderpatta or Indraprastha and
3. The then ruler of Indraprastha was Dhananjaya Korabya.

Another Kuru king named Ucchaisravas, uncle of King Kesin Dalbhya of Panchala is mentioned in the Taittiriya and Jaiminiya Brahamanas to have been ruling Kuru kingdom from Indraprastha during invasion by the non – vedic Salwa tribe who defeated the Kuru kingdom. From thereon, there is no further information of any Kuru kings ruling from Indraprastha or Hastinapura in any subsequent literature. The Anguttara Nikaya, an ancient Buddhist text mentions Kuru as one of the 16 mahajanapadas of Bharatavarsha which means it did not cease to exist after the invasion either. It is just that its power got diminished and governing structure changed from monarchy to republic or gana – rajya.

Later texts such as Kautilya's Arthashastra refer the Kurus as Corporations or republic only.

The serpent race, Nagas as they are called finds mention in the epic prominently especially in the Khandava daha Upa Parva or chapters of the Adi Parva which deals with displacement of this race from Khandava forest or vana which was burnt down from by Arjuna, (one of the five Pandava brothers) along with Lord Krishna to make way for establishing a new kingdom in its place, which was known as Indraprastha and corresponded to Delhi, west of river Yamuna. The royal palace, assembly hall and other structures built in the aftermath, details of which has been mentioned in the Sabha Parva of the epic at least attests to building of a new township in this area. Maya Danava or Asura who was caught in the Khandava forest fire was saved and in gratitude, he offered to build an assembly hall for the Pandavas, which he completed in 14 months.

Excerpts from Sabha Parva of the Mahabharata epic:
"The palace that Maya built consisted of columns of gold, and occupied an area of five thousand cubits. The palace possessing an exceedingly beautiful form, like unto that of Agni and Surya or Soma shone in great splendor, and by its brilliance seemed to darken even the bright rays of the sun. With the effulgence it exhibited, which was a mixture of both celestial and terrestrial light, it looked as if it was on fire. Like unto a mass of new clouds conspicuous in the sky, the palace rose up coming into view of all. Indeed, the palace that the dexterous Maya built was so wide, delightful and refreshing and composed of such excellent materials, and furnished with such golden walls and archways, and adorned with so many varied pictures, and was withal so rich and well built, that in beauty it far surpassed Sudharna of the Dasarha race, or the mansion of Brahma himself.

Within the palace, Maya placed a peerless tank, and in that tank were lotuses with leaves of dark coloured gems and stalks of bright jewels and other flowers also of golden leaves. Aquatic fowls of various species sported on its bosom. Itself variegated with full blown lotuses and stocked with fishes and tortoises with golden hue, its bottom was without mud and its water transparent. There was a flight of crystal stairs leading from the banks to the edge of the water. The gentle breezes that swept along its bosom softly shook the flowers that studded it. The banks of that tank were overlaid with slabs of exquisite marble set with pearls. Beholding that tank thus adorned all around with jewels and precious stones. Many kings who came there mistook it for land and fell into it with eyes open. Many tall trees of various kinds were planted all around the palace. Of green foliage and cool shade, and ever blossoming, they were all very charming to behold. Artificial woods were laid around, always emitting a delicious fragrance. There were many tanks also that were adorned with swans and Karandavas and Chakravakas in the grounds lying about the mansion. The breeze bearing the fragrance of lotuses growing in water and ministered unto the pleasure and happiness of the Pandavas. Maya having constructed such a palatial hall within fourteen months reported its completion unto Yudhishtira.

Excerpts from Indraprastha by B.B.Lal (Archaeologist), 2021 (Contd):
"Such an elaborate gold pillared and gem studded assembly hall measuring ten thousand cubits in circumference, can be found by the poor archaeologist only in his dreams and not with his spade! At the same time he has to accept the construction of a township, whatever be its details."

Excavations at Purana Qila, Delhi

1. Period I: Associated with the Painted Grey Ware: circa 10th century B.C. to 8th century B.C.
2. Period II: Associated with the Northern Black Polished Ware culture (800 – 200 B.C.).

Unfortunately, in the trenches so far dug, no regular layers bearing PGW were found. Only stray shards were met with. But the very presence of this ware is significant since it shows that the regular PGW settlement is close by, from where these shards have come down. The work so far has remained confined to a part of south eastern sector of Purana Qila. If and when other areas are tapped, there is every possibility of regular PGW deposits being found.

Both Indraprastha and Kaushambi are central to dating Mahabharata war because while the former was a township built within 50 years before the great war, the latter was built within 50 years after the war and populace in and around Hastinapura (after the Gangetic floods) settled within 100 years of the establishment of this new township. It is to be noted that Vatsa kingdom or its capital Kaushambi does not find mention in the Mahabharata epic, pointing to the fact that this township came into existence only after conclusion of the war and its immediate aftermath period mentioned in the epic.

Since, only a part of the south eastern sector of the Purana Qila (or ruins of Indraprastha fort) has been excavated and only stray shards have been found as a consequence, we can presume or at least sincerely hope that in future if the close by regular PGW settlement is found during excavations in other parts of the fort, then it will push Period I PGW culture there by at least two and a half centuries i.e. at least till 1250 B.C.

Excavations of the Kaushambi Fortifications or Mudwall

Excerpts from Kausambi Revisited, by B.B. Lal (Archaeologist), 2017:

The impressive fortification at Kaushambi in the Central Ganga basin – an enormous mud wall with a baked brick revetment extent to a height of as much as thirteen metres – has been thought to be structurally reminiscent of the defence-wall of Mound AB of Harappa.

As reported by G.R. Sharma (1957 -59) as many as 25 structural periods have been identified. These have been grouped under four major cultural periods, which have been dated as:

1. Kaushambi I, circa 1165 B.C.
2. Kaushambi II, circa 885 – 605 B.C.
3. Kaushambi III, circa 605 – 45 B.C.
4. Kaushambi IV, circa 45 B.C. – 580 A.D.

and the beginning of the fortification has been dated to circa 1025 B.C.

However, as per B.B. Lal, about the defence wall itself, it can be safely held that it is not as old as it has been held to be.

Although the 1165 B.C. date given in the "Excavations at Kaushambi, 1957-59 and Allahabad, 1960, by archaeologist G.R. Sharma may not be held to be accurate, but we can surmise from the findings that the continuity of a township or settlement had been there from 1025 B.C. till advent of Mahajanapada age in 623 B.C.

In short, archaeological evidence prove the existence of ancient townships of Indraprastha and Kaushambi from 10th century B.C. and also occurrence of the Hastinapura floods mentioned in the Puranas.

Image of the mud wall fortifications, Kaushambi, Sharma, 1960 (above).

CHAPTER 4
THE SINAULI CHARIOT

Excerpts from "The Sarasvati Civilization, by Maj Gen (Retd) G.D. Bakshi, 2019":

In 2018, the Archaeological Survey of India (ASI) made a startling discovery in Sinauli in Baghpat district, U.P. They stumbled upon the remains of a war chariot that dated back to around 1900 B.C. (thus predating the Iron Age of Bharatavarsha and in the process Mahabharata too). SK Manjul, Director, Institute of Archaeology and Arun Manjul, his deputy said, "The new finding will shed light on India's place in the ancient world history".

This is the first time chariots have been discovered alongside royal burial pits. These were certainly warriors. Archaeologists have recovered swords with copper covered hilts and a medial ridge that made it strong enough for war fighting. Shields, torches and daggers have also been discovered.

Toy Chariots in bronze and terracotta had been discovered much earlier but this is the first time a full blown war chariot has been discovered along with swords and daggers. The problem is that in the Indian tropical climate, it would be very difficult to preserve wooden chariots for very long. Nevertheless, one of the Holy grails of colonial historiography has been located at long last.

Image of the Sinauli Chariot (above).
Reconstructed Image of the Sinauli Chariot (below).

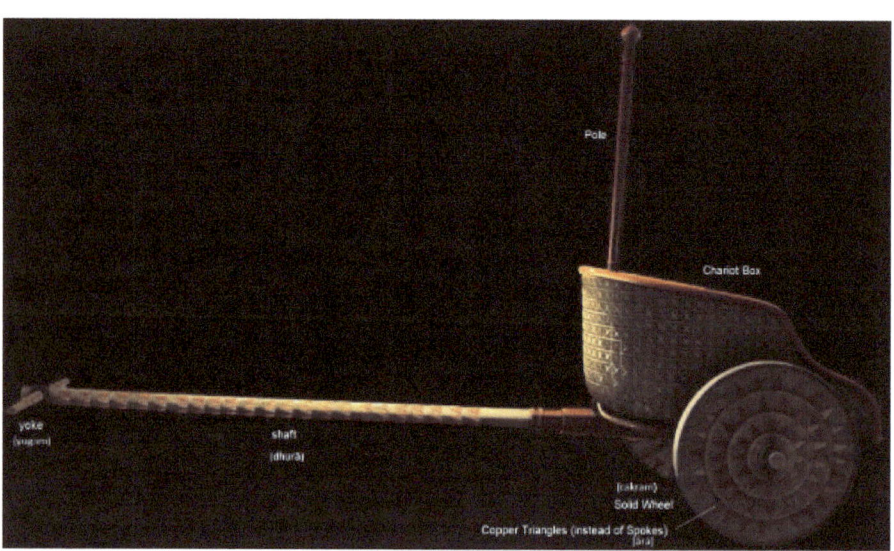

PART IV
FROM AN ASTROLOGICAL PERSPECTIVE

CHAPTER 1

THE DATE OF MAHABHARATA WAR AS PER VEDANGA JYOTISHA AND KOLLAM ANDU

Excerpts from "The Chronology of Ancient India", by Velandai Gopala Aiyer, 1901:

The archaic language in which our Vedanga is written and the unintelligible nature of some of the verses prove beyond doubt that it is a very ancient treatise, though perhaps not as old as the astronomical position it indicates. The ancient Aryans in India had a knowledge of elementary astronomical phenomena as is evident from the numerous references to them in the Rig and the other Vedas. To better enable them to fix the seasons for their innumerable sacrifices, they devised a few elementary treatises on astronomy, one of which is still preserved to us in the Vedanga Jyotisha.

Says Dr. M. Haug in his introduction to Aitareya Brahmana, "A regulation of the calendar by such observations was an absolute necessity for the Brahmans; for the proper time of commencing and ending their sacrifices, principally the so called 'Satras' or sacrificial sessions could not be known without an accurate knowledge of the time of the sun's northern and southern progress. The knowledge of the calendar forms such an essential part of the ritual that many important conditions of the latter cannot be carried out without the former."

Professor Max Muller admits that there must have been a real tradition which formed the basis of the astronomical positions recorded in the Vedanga Jyotisha. It states that the winter solstice occurred with the sun in the beginning of Dhanishta and the summer solstice took place with the Sun in the middle of Aslesha.[6] Consequently, the vernal and autumnal equinoxes occurred with the sun in the end of third pada of Bharani and in the end of the first pada of Visakha respectively. We do not find in the Vedanga any division of the ecliptic into 360 degrees; this is but natural, because in those early times such scientific divisions could not have been known. The treatise is familiar with the division of the heavens into 27 Nakshatras and probably

---

[6] Vedanga Jyotisha (Yajur recension), v.7.

also with division of each Nakshatra into four Amsas or quarters. Indeed this old kind of division of a Nakshatra into four Amsas is referred to in the following shlokas of the Vishnu Purana, II, 8:

प्रथमे कृत्तिके भागे यदा भास्वान्तदा शशी ।
विशाखानां चतुर्थांशे मुने तिष्ठत्यसंशयं ॥
विशाखानां यदा सूर्यश्चरत्यंशं तृतीयकं ।
तदाचंद्रं विजानीयात्कृत्तिका शिरसि स्थितं ।
तदेव विषुवाख्यो वै कालः पुण्योऽभिधीयते ॥

"When the sun, O sage is in the first quarter of Krittika and the moon is in the fourth quarter of Visakha or when the sun is in the third quarter of Visakha and the moon is in the head of Krittika, that it is the time of the equinox and it is holy."

Mr Wilson seems to have misunderstood the meaning of 'Bhaag' and 'Ansh' in the above verses, for he takes them to mean 'degree'. It will readily appear that 'quarter' is the more appropriate meaning for it is only then that the sun and moon are in "opposition" to each other.

The positions given by the Vedanga Jyotisha are also referred to by Garga and Varahamihira; but they differ from those obtaining at present and even from the positions mentioned by Varahamihira as been observed about the year 3600 (Warren's Kala Sankalita, p. 389) of the modern astronomical Kali era or in 499 A.D.

This great astronomer who was born in 505 A.D., says in his Brihat Samhita:

"In the old treatises it is said that the summer and winter solstices took place with the sun in the middle of Aslesha and in the beginning of Dhanishta respectively; but at present they occur in the beginning of Cancer (beginning of last quarter of Punavarsu) and of Capricorn (beginning of the second quarter of Uttarashada) respectively." Therefore the winter solstice, which happened with the sun in the beginning of Dhanishta at the time denoted by the Vedanga, had receded in 499 A.D., to the end of first quarter of Uttarashada, that is by an arc of 23° 20'. As the rate of precession of the equinoxes is, according to the illustrious French savant M Le Verrier about

50.24" per annum, the point of time denoted by our astronomical treatise is about 1672 years before 499 A.D. or about 1173 B.C. Archdeacon Pratt and Bentley, both of whom had gone over the calculation, were of the opinion that the observations indicated 1181 B.C.

The next question is to ascertain what it was that took place about 1173 B.C. of such consequence as to induce the ancient astronomers to record the astronomical positions for the event. Mr R.C. Dutt states that 'tradition has it when the Vedas were compiled, the position of the solisitial points was observed and recorded to mark the date.'

Professor Weber considers that both the Yajur Veda Samhitas may be shown from internal evidence to have assumed their present shape about the time of the war of the Mahabharata and the Puranas relate that Vyasa, the compiler of the Vedas, lived about the time of the war. It is therefore probable that the astronomical positions refer to the period of the war which preceded the beginning of the Kaliyuga by a few years. The Jyotisha itself states that the first year of the 'Yuga' commenced at the winter solstice with the sun and moon at the beginning of Dhanishta. In those early times, there were two kinds of 'Yugas' the five year cycle and the Kaliyuga [Vedanga Jyotisha (Yajur Recension), verses 5-7, Aitareya Brahmana VII – 15]. It is hard to believe that the positions referred to in the Vedanga denote only the beginning of such a short lived Yuga as the five year cycle. It is reasonable to suppose that they also mark the time of the commencement of the Kali with which probably began the first of a new series of five year cycles.

But it may be asked what authority there is, besides the Vedanga, to suppose that the Kali era began when the vernal equinox occurred with the sun in Bharani 10°. On the contrary, there seems to exist sufficient evidence to suppose that at the time of the Great war, which occurred a few years before the kaliyuga began, the vernal equinox took place with the sun in the Krittikas. For example, there are many passages in Taittiriya Samhita, the Taittiriya Brahmana and other Vedic works where the Krittikas occupy the first place[7] in the list of the Nakshatras. The Krittikas are the mouth of the Nakshatras, says the Taittiriya Brahmana (1.1.2.1). In the Atharvaveda (1.19.7) and in the Yagnavalkya – smriti, they occupy their early position, while the Vishnu Purana, as we have seen, actually places the vernal equinox in the beginning of the Krittikas. The Mahabharata says that the winter solstice took place sometime after the conclusion of the war on the fifth day after the new moon in the month of Magha and Hindu astronomers hold

---

[7] *Max Muller's Rig Veda, Vol IV Preface, p XXVII.*

from such references that the vernal equinox was then in the Krittakas (Mr Tilak's Orion, p.37 footnote). If therefore at time of the war, the equinox was in the Krittikas, it might appear that at the beginning of the Kali era, which very shortly followed the war, the vernal equinox could not have receded to Bharani 10°, that is a precession of 3°. 20' which would have taken about 240 years to be accomplished. But this difficulty is easily explained.

It must be remembered that though the astronomical treatise gives only 27 Nakshatras, the admittedly older works, the Atharva Samhita and the Taittiriya Brahmana enumerate 28 Nakshatras. What is more important is the fact that the list of the Atharvaveda connects the 28 Nakshatras with as many days and that the lists of the Taittiriya Brahmana show the connection of these 28 asterisms with a lunar synodical month. We may therefore infer that at the time of the compilation of these two Vedic works, the number of lunar asterisms was 28. But curiously enough, we meet with only 27 Nakshatras in the Taittiriya Samhita where Abhijit is left out. So, also the mention of 'trinava', 27 in the Taittiriya Samhita (VII.1.3.2) refers probably to 27 Nakshatras. While on the one hand the Taittiriya Samhita is the oldest of these three nearly contemporaneous compilations, the list of Taittiriya Brahmana on the other hand, mentioned in connection with an old kind of sacrifice called Nakshatreshti, a ceremony based upon the presumption that there were 28 Nakshatras. If we may judge by the generally received opinion that whatever is used for sacrificial purposes has the flavor of antiquity in it, possibly the original number was 28; and the mention of only 27 Nakshatras in the Taittiriya Samhita may be due to the fact that it was compiled under the immediate direction of the learned son (Vyasa) of a great astronomer (Parasara), the reputed author of an ancient astronomical treatise, who might have been the first to omit Abhijit from the list of the Nakshatras in order to suit his astronomical calculations. Professor Whitney and M. Biot hold that the original number was 28, while Professor Max Muller thinks that the Nakshatras was originally 27 (Rig Veda Vol IV, Preface Xlvi). For our present purpose, it is enough to note that at the beginning of the Kaliyuga, when the compilation of the Taittiriya Samhita, at least in its original form, was completed and that of the Brahmana was almost begun, people were acquainted with both the lists. But from that time forward astronomers continued to use 27 Nakshatras only. From the earliest astronomical treatise known to us, namely the Vedanga Jyotisha, to the latest work on Hindu astronomy, we find that all the Hindu astronomers Garga, Aryabhata, Varahamihira, Brahmagupta, Bhaskaracharya and many others regulate their calculations by the 27 Nakshatra system. It is this number that is referred to in the Mahabharata, Manu Smriti and the Vishnu Purana. We may therefore be sure that the number of 28 Nakshatras which prevailed about the time of Atharvaveda Samhita and of the Taittiriya Brahmana was not adopted by later astronomers who preferred to use the more astronomically suitable 27 Nakshatras.

The astronomers effected another improvement on the old method. The Nakshatras were made to begin with Dhanishta instead of with the Krittikas as of old. Somakara quotes an old saying of Garga in his commentary on the Vedanga Jyotisha (verse 5), तेषां च सर्वेषां नचत्राणां कर्मसु कृत्तिका: प्रथममाचक्षते श्रविष्ठातु संख्याया: ।, which means that

"Of these Nakshatras, the Krittikas are the first for sacrificial purposes and the Sravishta (Dhanishta) are the first for purposes of calculation." It is clear therefore that in those early times referred to by Garga, the 27 Nakshatras were counted from Dhanishta in works of astronomy. If the winter solstice was in the beginning of Dhanishta according to the Vedanga Jyotisha, the vernal equinox would be placed by astronomers in the end of the third quarter of Bharani. On the other hand, according to the 28 Nakshatra system, if the winter solstice be at the same place i.e. in the beginning of Dhanishta, the vernal equinox will occur with the sun in the beginning of the Krittikas. The same point in the heavens which according to the 27 Nakshatra system, denoted the end of the third pada of Bharani, also indicated the beginning of the Krittikas according to the 28 Nakshatra system. It is therefore wrong to suppose as scholars (according to Mr Tilak's Orion, p. 215) have hitherto done, that the beginning of the Krittakas mentioned in the Vedic works, denoted a point 3°20' removed from the end of third quarter of Bharani, mentioned by the Vedanga as the position for the vernal equinox. Thus, the positions given in the Vedanga are the same as those indicated in the Vedic works, noticed at the time of the war and recorded in the Vishnu Purana. The Vedanga Jyotisha itself confirms this inference as in enumerating the deities presiding over the various Nakshatras. It begins the list with Agni, the deity of the Krittikas and not with Yama, the presiding devata of the Bharani Nakshatra.

There is still another difficulty to encounter. It may be asked with reason how at such early times such an imaginary point in the heavens as the end of the third quarter of Bharani, without any star to denote the position, could have been supposed to mark the vernal equinox. To answer this question, this part of the heavens must be clearly laid before the mind's eye. Mrigasiras or the head stars of Orion are the earliest recorded beginners of the year in the very earliest period of Aryan history (Mr Tilak's Orion, Chapters IV, V, VI and VII). According to the Surya Siddhanta, Chapter VIII, the distance between the asterisms Mrigasiras and Rohini (Aldebaran) is stated to be 13°30'. The distance between the Rohini and the Krittikas and between the latter and Bharani are stated to be 12° and 17°30' respectively. As in those early times the heavens were divided into Nakshatras and Nakshatrapadas, and not into degrees and minutes, it must have been then crudely supposed that the distances between Mrigasiras and Rohini and between Rohini and the Krittikas represented nearly the arc covered by a divisional Nakshatra (i.e. 13°20') that the distance between the Krittikas and Bharani denoted a divisional Nakshatra and that the distance between the Krittikas and Bharani denoted a divisional Nakshatra and a quarter. The divisional Mrigasiras would therefore begin with the asterism Rohini (Aldebaran) and the divisional Rohini with the asterism Krittikas (Pleiades). The end of the divisional Krittikas would consequently coincide with the asterism Pleiades and its beginning would be placed about a pada after the asterism Bharani. Thus, the position given by the Vedanga Jyotisha for the vernal equinox, namely the end of the third pada of Bharani, was sufficiently identified as being distant from the stars Krittikas by one divisional Nakshatra and from the stars Bharani by one Nakshatrapada.

We may therefore conclude that, at the beginning of the Kaliyuga, the vernal equinox took place with the sun at the end of the third pada of Bharani. As it is recorded that in 499 A.D., the vernal equinox occurred with the sun in the first point of Aswina, there was a precession of 23°20' from the beginning of the Kali to 499 A.D.; that is in other words Kali era began about 1173 B.C. It consequently follows that it is unreasonable to suppose as some scholars have done, that the war happened about 1426 B.C. on the ground that the vernal equinox then took place with the sun in the Krittikas.

There are five important eras at present in use among Hindus in India of which the Vikrama and the Salivahana are the latest. The Saptarishi era is even now prevalent in Kashmir and the Kali is used generally in the rest of India. But the Malabar country is also guided by another era, called after

Parshurama, which is also known as Quilon or Kollam era. According to approved tradition, it is a cycle of a thousand years and the present cycle, believed to be the fourth, began in the year 1825 A.D. But curiously enough, Mr Logan thinks it to be an era beginning in 825 A.D., because no doubt that supposition suited his theory regarding the date of Cheruman Perumal, the supposed royal convert to Islam. Many scholars like Doctors Caldwell, Gundert and Burnell have tried to explain the true origin of Kollam Andu, but their explanations do not seem to be satisfactory. The late P.Sundaram Pillai, discussed these opinions in a paper contributed to the Madras Christian College magazine (Feb 1897) and finding them unsatisfactory suggested that the Kollam Andu was "a modification of another older era current in Upper India under the name of Saptarashya or Sastra Samvastara. The peculiarity of this northern era is that though it is today 1972, it is spoken of as 72 so that omitting the hundreds it would be found to be identical with our Malabar year except for four months beginning with Mesha." The Saptarishi begins with the month of Mesha; but the Kollam begins with Kanya in the north and Simha in the south of Malabar. Mr. Sundaram Pillai explains this divergence by supposing that in all probability the astronomers "found it necessary so to amend the northern luni – solar year in order to convert it into a purely solar one as the Kollam year professes to be." Mr. Sundaram Pillai, however ignores the fact of the Kollam Andu being a cycle and believes that it was adopted about 825 A.D. from the countries using the Saptarishi era. This is certainly a misconception and is due to the fact that the Kollam Andu at present counts the thousand years of the last cycle in addition to the expired years of the present cycle. Thus, the Kollam Andu for July 1901 is the 76th year of the fourth cycle; but it is now written as 1076 of the Kollam era. On the contrary, Lieutenant Col. Warren, who wrote his work Kalasankalita, just about the beginning of the present cycle in 1824 A.D., says of this Andu, "that there had expired on the 14th September 1800, two cycles of a thousand years each and 976[8] years of the third cycle". Mr R. Sewell states in his Indian Calender (P.45) that the years of the Kollam Andu "run in cycles of thousand years. The present cycle is said to be the fourth.

If there were really two cycles, ending with the year 1000, which expired 824-825 A.D., then it would follow that the Kollam era begin in Kali 1927 current or the year 3528 of the Julian period." Warren relied on a still earlier authority, Dr. Buchman, who stated "that the inhabitants of

---

[8] Must be 975 years. Kalasankalita p. 374. See Sewell's Indian Calendar, P. 45 footnote.

Malayala reckoned time in cycles of thousand years from 1176 B.C. and that in September 1800 A.D., there were two cycles and 976 years expired of that era."[9] We have therefore the authority of three eminent writers, two of whom lived before commencement of the present cycle, to the effect that the Kollam era is really a thousand year cycle beginning in August or September 1176 B.C.

Not only is the Kollam Andu a cycle of a thousand years, but it is also identical with the old Saptarishi cycle which is referred to by Alburini (1030 A.D.), Kalhana (1148 A.D.) and the Puranas. As many manuscripts in the Deccan College are said to be dated in the Saptarishi era, this era seems to have been more widely used than at present. Though the Kashmirians now state that this era began in 3076 B.C., it will be shown in a later chapter that about the time when the chronological portion of the Vishnu Purana was reduced to its present form, the Saptarishi era was supposed to begin a hundred years earlier, or in 3176 B.C., that the Vedic 'Saptarshichakra' cycle of a thousand years, the first cycle of which begins in 3176 B.C. and the second cycle of which ended in 1176 B.C., was the direct parent of, and was immediately followed by the modern Saptarshi kala. The Kollam Andu too is a cycle of thousand years and began in 1176 B.C. Is it not then most likely that both the Saptarshi and Kollam Andu cycles are almost identical? The earliest starting point for the modern Saptarshi Kala is the "birth of Parikshit when the Rishis were in Magha and the Kaliyuga then commenced" (Vishnu Purana). Thus, the Puranas identify the Saptarshi Kala with the Kaliyuga. As the Kollam era has been identified with the Saptarshi era, we may safely conclude that the Kollam Andu, the Saptarshi Kala and the Kaliyuga, all commenced in 1176 B.C.

The Kollam era seems to have been brought into Malabar by the Aryan Namburi immigrants at some remote period in the annals of southern India. "Everything about the Namburi society is hoary with age", says Mr. V. Nagam Aiya in his report on the Census of Travancore. What has been altogether forgotten by the Hindus in rest of India, Kashmir alone an exception, is still retained by these extremely conservative people of Malabar. But the very same reason which accounts for disappearance of this era in the rest of India, also contributed to the origin of the era being forgotten in Malabar. In the beginning of 6th century A.D., the astronomers made the Kaliyuga begin in 3102 B.C., and the authority of Aryabhata and Varahamihira was supreme enough to cause the spread of the new doctrine throughout the length and

---

[9] *Must be 975 years. Kalasankalita, p. 298*

breadth of India. The people of Malabar were therefore led to believe that the Kali began in 3102 B.C., connected their era, which really began with commencement of the Kali era in 1176 B.C. with the venerable name of Parashurama, the supposed leader of the Aryan immigration into Malabar. The Malabar Kollam Andu commenced in 'August or September', 1176 B.C. As the Vedanga Jyotisha, which refers to the period of the commencement of the Kaliyuga, begins the year with winter solstice (Yajur Vedanga Jyotisha, verses 6 and 7), we may well suppose that the Kaliyuga began with the winter solstice immediately preceding the commencement of the Kollam Andu or at end of 1177 B.C.

It is proposed in this chapter to examine fresh materials and to fix the date of the great Mahabharata war which was fought a few years before the beginning of the Kaliyuga. It is unanimously declared in the Mahabharata (Mahaprasthanika parva) and in all the Puranas that as long as Sri Krishna remained on earth, the Dwaparayuga continued and with his death commenced the Kali age. But the epic relates that the Pandavas left their kingdom soon after at the beginning of the Kaliyuga. The compiler of the epic wants us here to believe that the Kali commenced 36 years after the war. It is not safe to rely on every statement in the epic because it is neither the work of one author nor of one age.

On hearing his death (Lord Krishna's death), his devoted admirers, the Pandavas, did not care any longer to hold the reins of government, which indeed they would have already resigned, but that their grandson and heir, Parikshit had until then be too young to be trusted with the cares of an empire. The sweets of the purple had in fact never been acceptable to them, (Santi Parva), in as much as their victory was bought at too dear a price and only after a terrific carnage of all their dearest friends and relatives in the tremendous war. The death of Sri Krishna proved to be the proverbial last straw and the Pandavas once and for all determined to quit a world fraught with so many painful recollections. There is a pathetic fable current in Southern India that when Yudhishtira was ruling his empire with an even handed justice, he suddenly found on a certain day an unjust claim set up before him by a litigant who only the day before, had been pleading the cause of righteousness. The virtue monarch was astounded by this unprecedented and sudden decline in virtue and attributed it to the influence of the Kaliyuga, the dawn of which was then being expected. He forthwith resolved never more to witness the vices of the sinful age and having established Parikshit in the sovereignty of his realm, departed with his brothers on his grand Mahaprasthana. Whatever may be the reason that ultimately induced the Pandavas to retire from their worldly duties, it is evident that they were enabled to carry out their resolve the more easily by the fact that Parikshit had just then arrived at age. It has to be remembered that in precocious India, Hindu lawyers fix the age of majority in the sixteenth year. As Parikshit was born soon after the close of the war, the beginning of the Kali age, which is coeval with the coronation of Parikshit (Wilson's Vishnu Purana, Vol IV, p.232), must be placed about 16 years after the war; and if the Kali commenced in 1177 B.C. Parikshit must probably have been born in 1193 B.C. and the war should have taken place towards the end of the year 1194 B.C.

Concluding comments from author of this book:

King Parikshit was in his mother Uttara's womb at time of the Mahabharata war. Winter solstice happens on 21st December every year. If the Kaliyuga started around 21st December 1177 B.C. and Parikshit was 16 years at that time, then he would have been born towards end of 1193 B.C. The Mahabharata epic states that the winter solstice happened sometime after the conclusion of the war on the fifth day after the new moon in the month of Magha. The Magha month begins from 21st January and ends on 19th February every year. If the winter solstice happened around 21st January 1193 B.C., then the Mahabharata war should have indeed taken place towards end of the year 1194 B.C.

PART V

FROM A GEOLOGICAL PERSPECTIVE, SUPPORTED BY ARCHAEOLOGICAL EVIDENCE

CHAPTER 1

THE SAURASHTRA STONE ANCHORS – AN ARCHAEOLOGICAL SURVEY OF INDIA REPORT

Excerpts from Saurashtra Stone Anchors (Ring – Stones) from Dwarka and Somnath, Puratattva, ASI Bulletin No. 32, 2001-02:

Offshore explorations by the Marine Archaeology Centre of the National Institute of Oceanography, Goa brought to light a large number of stone anchors from Okhamandal region. The majority of stone anchors from Gujarat fall in three categories:

1. Composite
2. Grapnel
3. Ring Stone types

The last mentioned is a very enigmatic type as it is spheroid in shape with an axial hole and has been reported mainly from Gujarat coast; Dwarka and Somnath in particular.

Dwarka is situated in the Okhamandal taluka of Jamnagar district in Gujarat state on the extreme west of the Saurashtra peninsula on the Arabian Sea coast. Okhamandal region is separated from the rest of Saurashtra by the Okhla Rann.

Onshore excavations at Dwarka yielded an undisputed antiquity of the early historic period datable to 2nd century B.C. Offshore explorations have been carried out in Dwarka waters since 1983 and have brought to light a number of structures and anchors in water depths ranging between 3 and 15 meters. The sea – floor in Dwarka is represented by the occurrence of rocky cliffs, sandy patches and submerged river channel. The offshore contours of Dwarka suggest a gentle slope. Archaeological artefacts have been recovered near the rocky cliffs or found partially buried in sediments. A dense vegetation growth over the artefacts is observed up to 8 meter water depth. During fair weather, visibility is excellent for explorations and photography.

Results:

Offshore explorations at Dwarka and Somnath brought to light 133 and 43 different types of stone anchors respectively, besides a few stone structures in the Dwarka waters out of which ring – stones from Dwarka are 24 and 35 from Somnath. These ring stones have been collected in various field trips from the respective sites. The basic characteristics of these ring stone anchors are:

Circular in shape with an axial hole. Often the base of the ring stone is flat and top is semi – circular rising to a certain height. The detailed description of ring stones from Dwarka is given below:

Of the 24 ring – stones recovered from Dwarka waters, 11 were recovered up to year 2000 and remaining 13 in year 2001. Most of the ring stones were lying exposed on the sea bed. However, a few numbers were partially buried in the sediment. Up to a depth of 8 meter, often the exposed portion of the ring – stone are covered with marine growth such as sea weeds while ring – stones beyond this depth are covered with a thin layer of grayish marine growth. They are lying in a vertical position which is the normal falling position of this anchor on the sea bed and few ring – stones were marked. Some ring stones show chisel marks on the surface in the hole and on the flat bottom side. On the basis of materials and shapes, the ring – stones from Dwarka can be broadly divided into three groups:

1. Group I
   Six ring – stones fall in this group. The raw material used for this category is basalt and are heavy. The basic features are low height, flat bottom, semi – curved top with an axial hole; diameter of the hole is same at both ends. Often they are heavy and the average estimated weight of a ring – stone in this group is 147 kg. The weight of heaviest ring – stone is 245 kg and lightest is 80 kg.
2. Group II
   Thirteen ring – stones fall in this group. They are made out of two types of rocks i.e. limestone and sandstone. Shape of these ring stones is same as that of 1st category. However, they have often blunt edges and widened axial holes. The average estimated weight of these ring – stones of this group is 98 kg. The weight of heaviest ring – stone is 205 kg and weight of smallest ring – stone is 64 kg.
3. Group III
   Five ring – stones fall in this last category. They are made of porous limestone. As usual, they are circular in shape with comparatively less

height and have equal diameter on upper and lower side ends. Often axial holes are wide and irregular. The average estimated weight of these ring – stones is 66 kg. The heaviest anchor is weighing 109 kg and lightest anchor 20 kg.

A few facts about these objects (ring – stones) are given below:

1. These are man made objects and have not been found in association with any habitation sites in Somnath or Dwarka.
2. Their association with composite and grapnel stone anchors indicate that they were used for navigational purposes.
3. These ring – stones were often found in disturbed rocky sea – bed.
4. These anchors have been found in large numbers in the Saurashtra coast which seems to be the place of origin of these ring – stones.

Dating of these ring – stones would be speculative since they have not been found associated with any datable material.

Excerpts from Geological Significance of Stone Anchors from Dwarka waters, Gujarat, India by S.D. Iyer, K.H. Vora and A.S. Gaur, 2006:

Thermoluminesence (Vora, 2002) and radiocarbon dates (Gaur and Sundaresh, 2003) have helped to establish an age of about 3500 B.P. (before present) i.e. 1500 B.C. for the habitation at Bet Dwarka island.

The submerged structures of Dwarka, on their own have not been dated by any means i.e. direct, indirect or inferred. However, associated with these structures are some stone anchors (Rao 1987, 1990) which are similar to those found at Cyprus and Syria, the age of which is believed to be 3500 years B.P.

Excerpts from "An ancient harbour at Dwarka: Study based on recent underwater explorations" by A.S. Gaur, Sundaresh and Sila Tripathi, 2004:

Discovery of a large number of stone anchors suggest that Dwarka was an important port since the historical period and continued till late medieval period. Existence of a wide variety of anchors may suggest that different types and sizes of boats from different regions used to visit Dwarka harbor.

Conclusion from the Author:

The ancient city of Dwarka, now submerged was once a thriving port built in a natural harbour.

Image of Saurashtra ring – stone anchor.

CHAPTER 2

16 NOT 36 AND MAUSALA PARVA

After King Parikshit is born, the then Kuru king Dhritarashtra along with his wife Gandhari and Kunti (mother of Yudhishtira, Bheema and Arjuna) leave their palatial abode in Hastinapura for Vanaprastha i.e. dwelling in a forest as an ascetic or sanyasi in an Ashrama or hermitage.

Excerpts from Asramavasika Parva:

Dhritarashtra decides upon his hour of departure and summons the sons of Pandu. Along with Gandhari, he has had the minor rites of leave taking performed by Brahmanas proficient in the Vedas. Kunti walks ahead, leading Gandhari, whose eyes remain bound and whose hands is placed on Kunti's shoulder. Dhritarashtra walks confidently behind Gandhari, his hand on her shoulder. The ladies of the royal household, Dhrupada's daughter Draupadi, Subhadra of Sattwata vamsa, **Uttara, the daughter in law of the Pandavas, who has recently become a mother,** Chitrangada and others all accompany the old king, wailing like a flock of she – ospreys.

After finishing their ritual baths and prayers, from the banks of Bhagirathi river the aged sovereign, with his followers, all observing stern vratas, with their senses firmly restrained, make their way towards Kurukshetra. Dhritarashtra arrives at the ashrama of the Rajarishi Satayupa of profound wisdom and holds discourse with the sage, who was once a great king of the Kekayas, O parantapa.[10] Satayupa receives Dhritarashtra with due rites and honour. The two of them go together to Krishna Dwaipayana or Ved Vyasa's ashrama and there Dhritarashtra receives his diksha his initiation into Vanaprastha, the first stage of the spiritual life in the forest.

The Pandavas after Dhritarashtra's departure are afflicted by constant and heavy sorrow on account of their mother Kunti. Draupadi had lost all her children and the lovely Subhadra also has become childless. **However, when your grandsires look upon the son of Uttara, your father Parikshit, they somehow hold their prana in their bodies.**

---

[10] *Sage Vaishampayana narrating to King Janmajeya*

At Panchali's words, Yudhishtira summons all the commanders of his forces and says to them 'Let my army teeming with chariots and elephants prepare to march for I will go into the forest to see my uncle Dhritarashtra. To those who supervise the concerns of the ladies, the King gives the order: Let every manner of conveyance be well equipped and my thousands of closed palanquins. Let carriages and granaries, wardrobes and treasuries be prepared and ordered out and give our best mechanics the command to march. Let the men who have charge of our treasuries set forth towards the ascetic retreats of Kurukshetra.

The journey in slow marches with his contingent, Yudhishtira reaches Kurukshetra and then crossing the dark and holy Yamuna, sees finally at a distance, the ashrama of his uncle, the blind Rajarishi Dhritarashtra of deep wisdom. The Pandavas alight from their chariots and walk the rest of the way to Dhritarashtra's ashrama, bowing humbly. They are followed on foot by their Kshatriyas and soldiers, the people of the kingdom, and wives and women of the Kuru lords.

Yudhishtira and his brothers of lotus petal eyes sit themselves down in the ashrama of their uncle Dhritarashtra. Around him sit many hallowed ascetics from diverse realms who have come to the hermitage to catch sight of the broad chested Pandavas. They say, 'We want to know who amongst these is Yudhishtira, who are Bheema and Arjuna, who the twins and who is Draupadi of great fame.' The Suta Sanjaya points out the Pandavas naming each one and Draupadi, as well as the other ladies of the Kuru household.

Sanjaya says "This princess whose complexion is like that of molten gold, who sits with her child on her lap is Uttara, the daughter of King Virata (of Matsya kingdom).

Excerpts from the Chronology of Ancient India, by Velandai Gopala Aiyer, 1901:

The Mahabharata states that after expiry of fifteen years after the war, old Dhritarashtra left with his wife and Kunti for the forest glades to enable him to lead the holy life of a recluse. In the sixteenth year after the war, the Pandavas are said to have set out on a visit to these old people, taking with them all their male and female relatives. We are told that Uttara, the wife of Abhimanyu "who had recently become a mother" was also among the number "with her child (Parikshit) on her lap". It must be borne in mind that Parikshit was conceived sometime before the war, as he was son of

Abhimanyu who had lost his life in the war. The Mahabaharata in Sauptika parva expressly states that Parikshit was in Gremio Matris during the progress of the war. Consequently, he could not have been a baby at the breasts in the sixteenth year after the war.

Interpretations from both the above excerpts:
1. When King Dhritarashtra left his kingdom for the forest, Uttara, the daughter-in-law of the Pandavas had recently become a mother which means King Dhritarashtra went for Vanaprastha soon after King Parikshit was born i.e. one year after conclusion of the great war, not fifteen years after the war.
2. The Pandavas knew they have to rule the kingdom and hold 'Prana' in their bodies till Parikshit who was then a toddler grows up and comes of age.
3. The Pandavas visit them in their ashrama same year i.e. during second year after conclusion of the war, not during sixteenth year after the war as Sanjaya introduces princess Uttara to the ascetics of the hermitage as the princess with her child on her lap.

Excerpts from the Mausala Parva:

Construing the meaning of these omens of time, Krishna knows that the thirty sixth year has turned and that the words that Gandhari uttered, burning with grief at death of her sons and all her kinsmen, are about to come true. Entering the city of Dwaravati (Dwarka), Krishna says to his father Vasudeva, 'Do protect all the women of our house until Arjuna comes. Balarama waits for me at edge of the forest near the sea and I will meet him today. Today, I have beheld the annihilation of the Yadus, even as I saw the carnage of the Kurus, thirty six years ago.

Meanwhile, Daruka arrives in Hastinapura and tells those mighty Maharathas, the sons of Pritha, how the Yadavas had slaughtered one another with iron vajras created from the Rishi's curse. Hearing that the Vrishnis along with the Bhojas and Andhakas and Kukuras have all been slain, the Pandavas are stricken with anguish.

Then Arjuna, Krishna's beloved friend, bids his brothers farewell and sets out with Daruka for Dwarka to meet his uncle **Kunti's brother, Krishna's father. He predicts destruction will soon overtake the world.** Arriving with Daruka at Dwaravati, ocean city of the Vrishnis, the Kshatriya hero sees the once magnificent city looking like a widowed woman. The royal women of the city who had until then, the very Lord of the Universe as their protector, were now defenseless. Sixteen thousand of them had been Krishna's wives and upon seeing Arjuna they set up a loud lament. At last, Arjuna seeks out the mortal remains of Balarama and Krishna and has these cremated by men skilled at the task. He also had all others who had been slain in the fratricidal battle cremated and last rites performed. Thus, after duly and faultlessly performing the Sraddha rites for the dead Yadavas, Arjuna mounts his chariot and sets out for Indraprastha on the seventh day of his arrival.

The widows of the Vrishni heroes, wailing aloud follow the high souled son of Pandu in carriages and palanquins drawn by bullocks, mules and camels. It is a cavalcade of bleakness and grief. The servants of the Vrishnis, their horsemen and their chariot mounted guards too form part of the procession. At Arjuna's command, all the people of Dwarka and of the entire Anarta country, go with that stricken train, now comprising women, children and the aged, devoid of the Kshatriya heroes. No sooner have all Dwarka people left her walls and set foot on the mainland, then the sea, fathomless home of sharks and crocodiles, swells up in an inexorable tide and floods inundate Dwarka with all its vast wealth that her people could not carry along with them. The spectacle spurs the people of Dwaravati to lengthen their stride in fear, crying 'Ah ever mysterious is the course of fate!'

Having left Dwarka and seen her submerge and vanish forever, Arjuna makes his way by slow marches, frequently stopping in pleasant woods and hills and by refreshing streams so that Vrishni women can rest.

Excerpts from Mahaprasthanika Parva:

Hearing the particulars of the great slaughter of the Vrishnis, Yudhishtira sets his heart on leaving the world. The Pandavas resolute on retiring from the world in quest of punya, fetch Yuyutsu before them, Yudhishtira makes the Kuru kingdom over to the son of Dhritirashtra by his Vaishya wife Sukda.

Installing on the throne your father Parikshit in whose name the faithful Yuyutsu would rule until the young king was of age, the eldest Pandava, full of sorrow says to Subhadra, 'This son of your son will be the king of the Kurus.' The survivor of the Yadus, Krishna's grandson Vajra has also been made a king. Parikshit will rule in Hastinapura and the Yadava prince will rule in Indraprastha. To Yuyutsu he says "You must protect both of them equally and never set your heart on the path of adharma."

He calls together the people of Hastinapura, appoints the wise Kripa to be the Acharya and Guru to Parikshit and gives the young prince into his care to be his Sishya. When this is formally done, Yudhishtira summons all his subjects, the people of Hastinapura as well as those from the provinces, and tells them that he and his brothers intend to retire from the world.

Kripa and some others of importance stand around Yuyutsu who will now rule. The Pandava Mahatman and their queen Panchali of great fame observe the prescribed fast and set out with their faces towards the east. Walking on, those heroes reach the vicinity of the sea of red waters. Dhanajaya has not yet abandoned his celestial bow, the Gandiva, O king, nor his twin inexhaustible quivers, for he is still compelled by the attachment men have for their possessions they value most. There on the shore of western ocean, the Pandavas behold Agni Deva, the Fire God, barring their way like a hill asking them to give up the noble Gandiva and the twin quivers. Dhananjaya casts into the waves both the bow and the two quivers and Agni Deva, his task accomplished vanishes from before their eyes.

Now, the sons of Pandu turn their faces towards the south and journey in that direction (**Rann of Kutch was under water and part of Arabian sea at that time).** Along the coast of salt sea, those princes of Bharata vamsa travel to the south – west, arriving where the wondrous and magnificent city of Dwaravati once stood, now vanished into the ocean deeps. Turning then to the north, those heroes continue their final yatra.

Conclusion:

The annihilation of the Yadava race due to fratricidal battle amongst them, subsequent submergence of the Dwarka city and Pandavas setting out for their final journey happened after King Parikshit turned 16 years of age i.e. in 1177 B.C., not 36 years after conclusion of the great war as written in Mausala Parva because of the following reasons:

1. Yuyutsu was appointed as a regent for both King Parikshit and King Vajra by Pandavas before they set out on leaving the world which points out to the fact that both King Parikshit and Vajra were minors at that time.
2. At the time of their departure, Pandavas placed King Parikshit under care of Kripacharya as his Sishya or disciple, appointing the wise Kripa to be

his Guru or teacher. This would not have happened if King Parikshit was 36 years of age, which again proves he had just arrived of age at that time.
3. There is no mention of King Parikshit's marriage before Pandavas final departure from their kingdom which proves he had not attained marriageable age i.e. was a minor at that time.
4. It has to be remembered that in precocious India, Hindu lawyers fix the age of majority in the 16th year.
5. The Pandavas were holding 'Prana' in their bodies to wait for Parikshit to come of age. When he did in 1177 B.C., given the wiping of Yadava race including their beloved friend Lord Krishna, it is unlikely that they would have ruled for another twenty years.

CHAPTER 3

1177 B.C. GEOLOGICAL UPHEAVALS AROUND THE WORLD AND NOT IN BHARATAVARSHA?

Some of the late bronze age civilizations which existed in 13th century B.C. are:

1. The Egyptian Civilization (The New kingdom).
2. Mycenaeans of Greece.
3. Hittites of Anatolia (modern day Turkey).
4. Minoans of Crete.
5. Kingdom of Cyprus.
6. Kingdom of Ugarit in northern Syria.

Their collapse in and around 1177 B.C. was due to combination of many factors, prominent among them was Geological factors such as Earthquakes, famines and droughts and secondly invasion or attack by Sea Peoples.

Excerpts from 1177 B.C. the Year Civilization collapsed by Prof. Eric H. Cline, 2021:

The warriors entered the world scene and moved rapidly, leaving death and destruction in their wake. Modern scholars refer to them collectively as "Sea Peoples", but the Egyptians who recorded their attack on Egypt never used that term, instead identifying them as separate groups working together; the Peleset, Tjekker, Shekelesh, Shardana, Danua and Weshesh – foreign sounding names for foreign looking people.

In 1177 B.C., as previously in 1207 B.C., the Egyptians were victorious. The Sea Peoples would not return to Egypt a third time. Ramses boasted that the enemy were "capsized and overwhelmed in their places". "Their hearts" he wrote "are taken away; their soul is flown away. Their weapons are scattered in the sea." However, it was a Pyrrhic victory. Although, Egypt under Ramses III was the only major power to successfully resist the onslaught of the Sea Peoples, New kingdom of Egypt was never the same again afterwards, most likely because of the other problems faced by the entire Mediterranean region during this period, as we shall see below.

Earthquakes

Let us begin with earthquakes. The idea that they caused, or might have contributed to the destruction of some of the Late Bronze Age cities has been around since the days of Claude Schaffer, the original excavator of Ugarit. He thought that an earthquake caused the final destruction of the city for he found visible indications that an earthquake had rocked the city in the distant past. Photographs from Schaffer's excavations for example show long stone walls knocked off kilter, which is one of the hallmarks of earthquake damage. However, current thinking on the subject puts the date of this earthquake at 1250 B.C. or thereafter.

Thanks to recent research by archaeoseismologists, it now seems probable that mainland Greece, as well as much of the rest of the Aegean and Eastern Mediterranean was struck by a series of eathquakes beginning about 1225 B.C. and lasting for as long as 50 years, until about 1175 B.C. The earthquake at Ugarit identified and described by Schaffer was not an isolated event; it was one of many such quakes that occurred during this time period. Such a series of earthquakes in antiquity is known as an "earthquake storm", in which a seismic fault keeps "unzipping" by unleashing a series of earthquakes over years or decades until all pressure along the faultline has been released. In the Aegean, earthquakes probably hit during the time period at Mycenae, Thebes, Pylos, Kynos, Lefkandi, the Menalion, Kastanas in Thessaly, Korakou, Profitis Elias, Gla as well as Tiryns and Midea.

And just as people are killed during the collapse of buildings and are buried in the rubble when an earthquake hits a populated area today, so too at least 19 bodies of people possibly killed in these ancient earthquakes have been found during excavations at the devastated Late Bronze Age cities.

However, we must concede that although these earthquakes would have undoubtedly caused severe damage, it is unlikely that they alone were sufficient to cause a complete collapse of society especially some of the sites like Ugarit were clearly reoccupied and at least partially rebuilt afterwards.

Climate Change, Drought and Famine

During the mid-13th century B.C., a Hittite queen (referred to only as "Puduhepa" – which is literally the Hittite word for "queen" rather than her personal name) wrote to the Egyptian pharaoh Ramses II stating, "I have no grain in my lands." Soon thereafter, probably in a related move, the

Hittites sent a trade embassy to Egypt in order to procure barley and wheat for shipment back to Anatolia.

An inscription of the Egyptian pharaoh Merneptah in which he states that he had "caused grain to be taken in ships, to keep alive this land of Hatti", further confirms that there was famine in the land of Hittites towards the end of thirteenth century B.C. and that a relief mission was sent by the Egyptians, just as today food is similarly sent to areas in need. Additional correspondence sent from the Hittite capital city attests to the ongoing crisis during the following decades, including one letter in which the writer rhetorically asks "Do you know that there was a famine in the midst of my lands?"

Some of the letters found at Ugarit in northern Syria also concerned with the transportation of large quantities of grain to the Hittites in Anatolia. One missive sent from the Hittite king to the King of Ugarit is concerned specifically with a shipment of two thousand units of grains (possibly as much as 450 tonnes). The Hittite king ends his letter dramatically stating, "It is a matter of life and death!"

Another letter is similarly concerned with the shipment of grain, but it also requests that many boats be sent as well. This led to the original excavators of Ugarit to hypothesize that it was a reaction to the incursions of the Sea Peoples, which it may or may not have been. Even the last king of Ugarit, Ammurapi received several letters from the Hittite king Suppiluliuma II in the early 12th century B.C., including one chastising him for being late in sending a much needed shipment of food to the Hittite homeland. That was sent sometime in the years just before the final destructions of both the Hittite kingdom and Ugarit, and declared plaintively "The Sun himself (i.e. the Hittite king) is perishing."

Itomar Singer of Tel Aviv University in his estimation, the evidence both textual and archaeological, indicates that "climatological cataclysms affected the entire eastern Mediterranean region towards the end of second millennium B.C."

One of the letters found in the House of Urtenu at Ugarit in northern Syria refers to a famine ravaging the city of Emar in inland Syria at the time it was destroyed in 1185 B.C. The letter was sent by someone named Banniya (or Eniya), who worked for Urtenu's commercial firm but was stationed in a branch office located in Emar. The relevant lines contains a stark message: "There is a famine in your (i.e. our) house; we will all die of hunger. If you do not quickly arrive here, we ourselves will die of hunger. You will not see a living soul from your land."

Additional texts, including some published as recently as 2016, shows that even the Ugarit itself was affected by famine. One is a letter sent from the Egyptian pharaoh Merneptah to the King of Ugarit, which was found in the house of Urtenu; it states explicitly that there was famine in the city. In the letter, the pharaoh cited an earlier letter and quoted the words of Ugaritic king back to him: "So, you had written to me: '(In) the land of Ugarit there is a severe hunger. May my lord save (the land of Ugarit) and May the king give grain to save the life……and to save the citizens of the land of Ugarit.'" As Yoram Cohen, an Assyriologist at Tel Aviv University, has pointed out, in response to this plea from the Ugaritic king, the pharaoh sent gold objects, large amount of textiles and seven thousand dried fish (of various sorts).

The chastising letter sent from the Hittite king Suppiluliuma II to Ammurapi of Ugarit near the end of life of the city, cited above similarly says, "You have sent a message……to the effect that there is no food in your land." In another letter, an unnamed king of Ugarit wrote to an unidentified, but probably royal and senior correspondent, saying bluntly, "(Here) with me, plenty (has become) famine", while in yet another an Ugarit official said to the King of Ugarit, "Another thing my lord: grain staples from you are not to be had! (The people of) the household of your servant will die of hunger! Give grain staples to your servant!"

There is also a text sent from the King of Tyre, located in the coastal area of what is now Lebanon, to the King of Ugarit. It informs to the Ugaritic king that his ship which was returning from Egypt loaded with grain had been caught in a storm: "Your ship that you sent to Egypt, died (was wrecked) in a mighty storm close to Tyre. It was recovered and the salvage master [or captain] took all grain from the jars. But I have taken all their grain, all their people and all their belongings from the salvage master [or captain], and I have returned (it all) to them. And (now) your ship is being taken care of in Akko, stripped." In other words, the ship had either sought refuge or been successfully salvaged. Either way, the crew and the grain were safe and were awaiting the command of Ugaritic king. The ship itself, it seems, was berthed in the port city of Akko.

"Timeline" for the final decades of Ugarit, although precise dates for the order of the events are not possible:

1. Ugarit happily interacts with foreign powers (e.g. trade with Egypt).
2. Earthquake damages city, but does not destroy it.

3. Ugarit sends aid relief (grain) to Hittites.
4. Famine descends on city.
5. Egypt sends aid relief (food, textiles etc.).
6. Enemy ships are spotted.
7. Enemy overruns nearby Ras Ibn Hani and threatens Ugarit.
8. City is destroyed in battle, leaving destruction debris two meters high.
9. City is not reoccupied for centuries.

We return, therefore, to the topic of drought which has recently been given new impetus as a result of additional findings published by scholars, working either individually or in teams in a number of different areas in the Aegean and Eastern Mediterranean. Their research has involved investigating the ancient pollen in Syria, Israel, Egypt and Cyprus; isotopic signatures and other indicators from lake sediments in Turkey, Syria and possibly Iran; oxygen isotope studies from stalagmites and mineral deposits within caves in Greece and Israel; and other relevant research.

Taken as a whole, the evidence now points conclusively to a drought in the region that lasted for 150 years and possibly 300 years, beginning about 1200 B.C. It may be more accurate to call it a mega drought, which is defined as "a severe drought that occurs a broad region for a long duration, typically multiple decades."

As written in Excerpts from Mausala Parva in previous chapter, Vasudeva father of Lord Krishna had rightly predicted that 'Destruction will soon overtake the world'. **Submergence of Dwarka city in Bharatavarsha could have very well happened in 1177 B.C. preceding the beginning of Kaliyuga which began with the winter solstice immediately preceding commencement of Malabar Kollam Andu or at the end of 1177 B.C.**

CONCLUSION

1177 B.C. was a year of Geological Upheavals around the world which have been discussed in the previous chapter and in the book '1177 B.C. The Year Civilization Collapsed by Professor Eric H Cline, 2021. Earthquakes, famines and droughts led to collapse of many Late Bronze Age civilizations in and around Mediterranean.

Submergence of Dwarka city in Bharatavarsha could have very well happened in 1177 B.C. preceding the beginning of Kaliyuga which began with the winter solstice immediately preceding commencement of Malabar Kollam Andu or at the end of 1177 B.C.

The Malabar Kollam Andu as discussed in detail in Part IV Chapter 1 of this book commenced in 'August or September', 1176 B.C.

King Parikshit was in mother Uttara's womb at time of the Mahabharata war. Winter solstice happens on 21st December every year. If Kaliyuga started around 21st Dec 1177 B.C. and Parikshit was 16 years of age at that time, then he would have been born towards end of 1193 B.C.

The Mahabharata epic states that the winter solstice happened sometime after the conclusion of the war, on the fifth day after the new moon in the month of Magha. The Magha month begins from 21st January and ends on 19th February every year. If the winter solstice happened around 21st January 1193 B.C., then **the Mahabharata war should have indeed taken place towards end of the year 1194 B.C.**

BIBLIOGRAPHY

1. 1177 B.C. The Year Civilization Collapsed by Professor Eric H Cline, 2021.
2. Ajatshatru The Great King of Magadha by Kapil Kapoor, 2018.
3. Ancient Indian Coinage by Rekha Jain, 1995, reprinted 2017.
4. Indraprastha by B.B. Lal, 2021.
5. Kausambi Revisited by B.B. Lal, 2017.
6. Marvels of Indian Iron through the Ages, by R. Balasubramanium, 2008.
7. The Complete Mahabharata (12) by Manjulika Dubey, 2017.
8. The Chronology of Ancient India by Velandai Gopala Aiyer, 1901.
9. The Earliest Buddhist Shrine: Excavating the birthplace of the Buddha, Lumbini (Nepal) – R.A.E. Coningham, K.P. Achary and others, 2013.
10. www.vyasaonline.com
11. Wikipedia.
12. The Saraswati Civilization by Maj Gen (Retired) G.D. Bakshi, 2019
13. Kautilya's Arthashastra by Shri Rudrapatna Samasastri, 1909.
14. The Origins of Iron Working in India: New evidence from the Central Ganga Plain and the Eastern Vindhyas by Archaeologist Rakesh Tewari, Antiquity, 2003.
15. Saurashtra Stone Anchors (Ring – Stones) from Dwarka and Somnath, Puratattva, ASI Bulletin No. 32, 2001-02.

www.ingramcontent.com/pod-product-compliance
Lightning Source LLC
LaVergne TN
LVHW070939070526
838199LV00039B/721